A WILD RIDE:

The Plan that Changed Everything

A WILD RIDE:

The Plan that Changed Everything

Randy Koons

IRIS STUDIOS

A WILD RIDE: The Plan that Changed Everything

Published 2020 in the US by Iris Studios, LLC

Email: a-wild-ride@irisstudios.com

Blog: www.a-wild-ride.com

ISBN-13: 978-1736310007

Cover illustration and design by Randy Koons

Acknowledgment

I've been writing for many years in different forms and genres, from fantasy to memoir and technical papers to short stories. My memoir, *A Wild Ride: The Plan that Changed Everything*, is the first long-form work I've completed and published and the first in my memoirs series. It's been a long process, and I couldn't have reached this point without many people's invaluable help.

Perhaps my work's primary editorial influence has been my involvement with the Writer's Group, sponsored by the Keene Public Library in Keene, New Hampshire. This is a read-and-critique process that I've run for over seven years. The improvement to my writing has been significant after interacting with dozens of other writers whose feedback and critique have been essential.

Several members of the Writer's Group have been gracious enough to be beta readers for this memoir. I appreciate that they took the time to read and comment, providing crucial editorial input. My special thanks to Denise, John, and Lou-Anne for all their help.

Finally, no acknowledgment would be complete without thanking my wife. MaryBeth has encouraged my writing as I have encouraged hers. She has given me the time to pursue my writing. Additionally, she has been a super-beta reader, as she helps me during the writing process. It's a great help to display my files on the big-screen TV, and together we read, and she provides editorial and creative input. It's wonderful to share this experience with my wife of 35-years, and without her valued support, I never would have finished this memoir.

Introduction

It's all in the telling. I'm just a regular guy who's entertained friends, relatives, coworkers, and others by sharing stories of my adventures. In recent years, I've committed some of them as short written memoirs and shared them with a group of other writers. Recently I decided to present them in a series titled *A WILD RIDE* as it aptly describes my life.

Memoirs are personal recollections of events based on unique perspectives and experiences. A dozen people can witness the same event yet tell a dozen different versions of what happened. This memoir is my version of the best recollections of real people, places, and events, and it's full of dialog because good dialog makes for good storytelling. I use reconstructed dialogue to convey the flavor of conversations and relate true stories of my life, which allows me to present events with a dramatic and comedic touch to create a more engaging experience.

The Plan that Changed Everything is the first installment in this series of memoirs. I chose it because it stands as the pivotal event in my life. Sure, there are other candidates for that distinction, but The Plan is the clear winner. I was twenty-five when this story began to unfold, so I'm not starting at the beginning of my life. The contexts that form the foundation of this story can't fit within this memoir, leaving much for the subject of future stories titled *A WILD RIDE*. However, let me provide some background information to make more sense of *The Plan that Changed Everything*.

◈

I grew up in the 50s and 60s in suburban Stamford, Connecticut, not far from New York City. I was the youngest of three kids with two sisters, five and seven years older than me. My mother was a stay-at-home mom, my father struggled as an advertising account executive and copywriter, so money was usually tight. "Money is nothing," my father would proclaim. "Family is everything." His other mantra, "I'll never tell you kids what to do with your lives. Just don't go into advertising." That's about the extent of my parental advice to prepare me to become an adult.

My parents never finished college but were well-read and keenly interested in history and natural science. During World War II, my father learned and then taught celestial navigation to Navy pilots, and later became a celestial navigator with Air Transport Command. Before I was born, my father was an advertising account executive. They were into fishing, camping, and mineral collecting. We went on long camping trips in New England, out west, and in Canada, so I spent a lot of time out of doors.

My sisters were well behaved in school, did their work, and stayed out of trouble.

Not me. I got into trouble early off. I didn't do my schoolwork, was a disciplinary problem, became a class clown starting in first grade. I set my closet on fire and got busted for pulling false alarms and shoplifting in second grade. In fourth grade, I swiped my father's unregistered WWII souvenir submachinegun to run around the neighborhood playing army with my friends. In fifth grade, I handed out live ammunition to my elementary school pals and was busted again for shoplifting. When in junior high, I made explosives.

I may not have done my homework or reading assignments; yet, I studied a Van Nostrand's Scientific Encyclopedia, Time-Life nature and science volumes, Scientific American, and Sky and Telescope magazines. I constantly doodled and drew and was always thinking of different inventions, especially in class.

If I grew up in contemporary times, I'm sure I'd have been

diagnosed with Attention Deficit and Hyperactivity Disorder (ADHD). As it was, I spent many, many hours during elementary and junior high school with counselors and therapists. They kept telling me, "You're so smart, there's no excuse for not living up to your potential." Professional recommendations sent me off to an all-boys boarding high school. The experience yielded mixed results, but I never learned how to be a student. As a result, after I went to college at the University of Arizona in Tucson, I dropped out after a year as a Geoscience major. As soon as I left college, I started teaching myself to become a commercial artist and graphic designer. I'd worked as a maintenance man, freelance commercial artist, art director, and underground copper miner, but I'd never held a full-time job longer than six months.

I was not quite twenty-three years old, with no reliable means of support, when I married Kate, my first wife, a divorced woman, seven years my senior. She had three children from her first husband; the oldest boy was only fourteen years younger than me.

That's a thumbnail of my life before meeting Kate. It's who I was and what I brought to my marriage. These are many of the underlying elements that brought us to the moment when my story begins. Within this story, I'll cite other adventures that I'll cover in future memoirs. But for now, join me on *A WILD RIDE: The Plan that Changed Everything.*

Chapter 1

Stress

IT WAS DAMN COLD THE WINTER OF '78. The thermometer didn't rise above zero for 45 days straight in the tiny town of Marlow, New Hampshire, where I lived with my wife, Kate, and our kids. It was miserable outside and cold inside.

I spent seven months trying to get the old house we bought ready for that winter. I insulated some walls and put in a wood stove, but I was lucky to get the place up to 60-degrees during the winter, and between the wood stove in the living room and our wood-fired kitchen stove, there was a persistent smell of smoke. The house, built in 1840, had two rooms, a kitchen, and a bath on the first floor, and four small bedrooms upstairs.

Granted, it was still better than the old farmhouse with no indoor plumbing, where we lived two years earlier, during our experiment at a "hippy commune" called Hidden Springs. That hippy commune was more like some twisted socialist tenant farm. Having become disillusioned within six months, we fled to Marlow—the next town over.

In 1975, I had married Kate, seven years my senior, and recently divorced from her IBM executive husband. I was suddenly a stepparent to three kids—David (8), Michael (6), and Amy (4). After returning to Connecticut from Tucson, Arizona, I met Kate, where I'd been working as an underground copper miner. I was young, naïve, willing, and above all—a dumb 22-year-old.

As I was a struggling commercial artist and Kate had fled from suburbia, she and I thought it would be a wonderful idea to move the family away from it all, get back to nature, and find a community in the forests of New England. That's how we found Hidden Springs early in November '75. The crazy things some parents think—what a mistake.

Marlow is a little town in southwest New Hampshire. When we moved in, there were just over 400 residents. Employment opportunities in the region were terrible, and there was little work for my freelance commercial art. While at Hidden Springs, we cut and sold firewood to support the community. After we moved to Marlow, I took a contract job cutting cordwood, which paid poorly. Kate received child support from Charlie, the kids' father, but that didn't cover all their expenses. We lived under severe financial stress. Then in September 1976, my daughter Anne was born. I know, I know. What kind of moron has four kids when he couldn't afford three?

Kate and I wanted a big family. I took my role as a parent seriously and wanted children of my own. It seems crazy today, but people often look at history through the lens of current times, but that was a different era. We figured we could make it work. Well, we figured wrong and struggled to survive.

As 1977 came to a close, I was desperate for a better means to support my growing family. I had a graphics job for a short while, but that didn't work out. I found some freelance work, but there wasn't enough to support us. To survive, I went back to cutting cordwood and this time during the winter, working on snowshoes in subzero weather. It was grim and dangerous work.

I was miserable working in the woods that winter, but life in my house was crazy. The subzero temperatures kept the kids inside because outside, they'd have frozen. Anne was sixteen months old and teething up a storm. It seemed like she howled day and night, letting everyone know how miserable she was. David and Michael were two extremely rowdy twelve- and eight-year-old boys, with energy to burn and mischief in their hearts.

David loved to beat on Michael, and Michael loved to bait his older brother. They were like some sort of out-of-control perpetual motion machines, often engaging Toby, our 75-pound sheepdog mutt, into barking and chasing them through the house and up and down the stairs—floors shook, doors slammed, walls vibrated.

Unlike when we lived in Connecticut, where we picked up seven New York City TV stations, in Marlow, we barely received one channel. Of course, this was before streaming, DVDs, VCRs, and readily accessible cable TV. Therefore, television wasn't much of a distraction to capture the kid's attention and deliver rare periods of silence. It was madness that obliterated my diminished patience. One day, Michael pushed me over the edge. I grabbed him on the fly. I spun and twirled his body like a human baton with my powerful hands and arms as David watched in horror. I couldn't imagine life getting any crazier, but, once again, I was sorely mistaken.

Early in February, Kate discovered she was two-months pregnant. I was thrilled at the prospect of another child. After all, I'd been programmed by a father who repeatedly sold me a bill of goods with his mantra, "Money is nothing. Family is everything." Unfortunately, I was quickly discovering that without money, there could be no family.

Chapter 2

Worry

ONE FRIGID MORNING I WATCHED FOUR KIDS EATING BREAKFAST. At the other end of the table sat Kate, pregnant with a child due in September. I was worried. I was beyond worry; I was terrified. Calculating the cost of shoes alone was enough to make my skin crawl. I thought to myself, *What the hell am I going to do?*

I couldn't keep working in the woods. I couldn't find enough freelance commercial art, and there was no other decent employment anywhere nearby. I had to think of a workable plan to change my lot in life to support my family.

That afternoon, early in March, it snowed, and the boys were particularly wild. Anne was teething and let everyone in the house know it. The conditions inside and outdoors prevented me from meaningful thinking about how to solve my career problems. I thought my head would explode. Stresses and pressures were enormous, much like conditions that compress carbon to form diamonds. Somehow, concern about the cost of shoes was a catalyst with the pressure. Suddenly, my thoughts crystallized into a radically insane plan—and it scared me. I was afraid to tell Kate what thought had formed in my mind. *No way,* I thought. *This idea's beyond insane. If I suggest it, she'd probably kill me.* I had one option—suppress my thoughts and forget it.

Unfortunately, the next morning, faced with the same scene, I worried again how I could ever afford shoes. My mood grew dark and brooding.

After a morning of thunderclouds circling my head, Kate finally asked, "What the hell's going on with you?"

I spilled my fear of shoes. It came out as incoherent nonsense, which painted blank and confused expressions on Kate's face. She finally grasped my immediate concern and put the question to me, the one I'd grappled with the previous day, "Well, what are you going to do about it?"

Nervously, I stammered, "I … solved half the question … yesterday—"

"And!" Kate's patience evaporated.

Still, the answer was too bizarre to vocalize. I hemmed and hawed, verbally dancing around the large elephant standing in the corner—which, by the way, offered me no support. "I need something more reliable than cutting firewood or freelance art." I stalled, unable to reveal my crazy idea.

"That's not news." She pressed further as her anger fumed. "Just tell me what's on your mind."

Finally, I blurted out, "I can't figure out how to change my life. I can't think in this madhouse. There's too much commotion—"

"What are you talking about!"

I tried to explain calmly. Shock is a feeble description of her expression. Finally, she took a deep breath. "Tell me again," she spoke quietly, "I want to make sure I heard you correctly."

Even today, as I recall that moment, I'm stunned by my suggestion. I swallowed hard, maintained eye contact, and spoke very slowly, "To come up with a workable career plan, taking into account all the circumstances of my life, I have to get out of the house for a while." I paused as long as I dared, fearing the storm was about to break. "I need to go to Tucson so I can think of a plan."

Repeating my concept changed nothing in her dumbfounded expression. She just stared for a few moments. Then she posed a follow-on question. "And just how do you propose to get there and back?" Anger hardened her face. "We're broke…. And I'm pregnant!"

If my plan wasn't crazy enough, my next answer fell like a sledgehammer. "I'll hitchhike—"

"You're insane!" She hit the nail right on top of my pointy head.

"I must be. How else could I suggest hitchhiking over six-thousand miles?" I studied her face. "And leaving you here alone pregnant with the kids...."

I expected expletives and threats that if I went anywhere, it would be to a padded cell. But Kate just stared at me and said nothing, and then walked away. I felt lucky to have survived and thought, *I need a more practical plan.*

That night, just before we went to sleep, I discovered that insanity was contagious. Kate looked at me and said, "I've been thinking all afternoon and evening." Her voice was remarkably calm. "You do need a plan. If hitchhiking to Tucson and back will make that happen," she hesitated. "I think you should go." My mouth gaped with shock. "We both know you have to do something, and I don't have a better idea." She then got down to logistics. "Where will you stay in Tucson?"

"I'm sure my former roommate, Jack, will put me up." I felt confident about that, even before I asked him.

"How long will you be gone?"

I hadn't given that much thought, so I tossed out a number. "Four weeks." I was sure she'd negotiate me down on how long I'd be gone.

Silently, she knit her brows and considered it for a few moments and then said, "Okay."

I was stunned that Kate agreed to be left for four weeks, pregnant in our small house—still in the throes of winter—with three kids, and a teething baby, while I hitchhiked to Tucson. Turning off the light, she asked, "How soon can you leave?"

"A couple of days."

I lay in the dark, contemplating what was about to happen. *Now I've stepped in it. What have I gotten myself into?* What had started as a crazy idea had suddenly become a reality. In a few days, I'd be leaving my wife and family to hitchhike 3,000 miles to Tucson. *I must be crazy*. I was sure my parents would see this as a further descent into madness following my irresponsible marriage. Kate's father, who hated me, would be convinced I was running away from my family responsibilities—and he wouldn't be the only one who'd think that way.

That thought rolled around in my mind, depriving me of sleep. I had to ask myself, *Am I running away?* An immediate *NO* was my response. If I contemplated running out, I wouldn't be thinking of a roundtrip. I could never abandon my family. I loved them too much.

It was that love and responsibility that brought about this crazy scheme. I was falling farther behind financially, and I had to do something to better support my family. I wasn't running away. I was diving headlong into the deep-end of responsibility, like husbands and fathers before me. Off they went to the goldfields, went to sea, logging, or even immigrating to create better lives for their families. Those were harrowing and dangerous journeys fraught with sacrifice and deprivation in the desperate hope to strike it rich. When I came up with this scheme, it was for the sake of my family.

Chapter 3

Departure

I HAD HITCHHIKED AROUND TUCSON IN THE EARLY '70s, WHEN I DIDN'T HAVE A WORKING CAR, so I understood the game. However, local hitchhiking was one thing; traveling thousands of miles by thumb was something entirely different. When I proposed going to Arizona, there weren't nearly as many people hitching anymore. I was no stranger to traveling to Arizona. In the early '70s, I made four round trips driving between Connecticut and Tucson, so I knew my possible routes. Given the time of year, I ruled out crossing Nebraska to Colorado. I settled on heading south to I-40, which would take me from Tennessee to Arizona. I understood the enormous distances of the Plains states and the west. Faced with that reality, it made me nervous and scared. All my other trips, I drove and was in control of the route and the timing. This time I'd be at the mercy and kindness of strangers. I tried to ignore the more sinister possibilities that crept into my mind.

I had to pack light, but also for cold and hot weather. My pack frame and backpack contained clothes and other items, including sign making materials and an embroidery hoop and supplies. During the winter, I took to decorating my denim jacket with various embroidered designs. I assumed there would be many idle hours when I could work on my jacket. I also had to make sure enough firewood was available for the boys to bring inside.

The night before I left, dinner felt like the last meal of a condemned man. I don't think the kids understood what was going on, but Kate sat there in a somber mood. She still believed I should make the journey, though she too was nervous about our being apart. I told the kids how I'd leave in the morning and that they needed to help their mother while I was gone. I barely slept that night, and when I did, I had nightmarish visions of being stranded along the road in the middle of nowhere.

◈

Early the next morning, I rose and shaved, knowing my face wouldn't feel a razor until I reached Tucson. Staring back from the mirror, I saw shoulder-length brown hair parted in the middle that flowed behind my ears, framing my face as I applied the shaving lather. I never could grow a good beard, but my thick droopy mustache had been on my face for seven years, which gave me a sort of stern expression. I dressed, pulling on my jeans, and lacing my hiking boots, preparing for the expedition. As I buttoned a gray flannel shirt and pulled on my maroon sweater, I knew I'd be on the road for several days, wearing the same clothes. I went downstairs and ate a big breakfast, as I didn't know when I'd have my next meal.

Kate and I didn't say much before slipping into my long gray trench coat and then completed the ensemble with a floppy brown wide-brimmed felt hat. I felt like an old-west prospector heading for the goldfields to seek my fortune. I suppose back then; I didn't look too oddly dressed. Standing six-one, with a lean but muscular body from working in the mines and the woods, I felt my size would ensure my safety. I regarded the family one last time, then hugged the kids' goodbye, grabbed my pack, and headed to the van with Kate.

"I put some water, a sandwich, and snacks in your bag," Kate said as she started the green Dodge van.

"Thanks. I appreciate that." I felt nervous at the unknown that lay ahead and concerns for my family left behind.

As Kate turned onto Rt. 10 and headed toward Keene, she asked, "Do you think forty dollars will be enough?" Forty dollars back then was worth about $160 in today's money.

"It'll have to be, 'cause I can't afford to take any more. I'll eat cheap when I'm on the road, and Jack said he'd feed me when I stay at his place." We continued in silence to Keene, some ten miles away. We were both lost in our thoughts of the weeks to come.

Kate dropped me off on Rt. 9 just west of Keene, which headed west to Vermont, where I'd catch I-91 south. The day was clear but cold when I emerged from the car with my backpack. We said our goodbyes, and I promised to return safely in four weeks with a workable plan to transform our finances and lives. "I'll hold you to it," she said flatly. We exchanged brief hugs and kisses, and then she got in the van and pulled away, leaving me alone, standing by the road. It was 7:30 a.m.

My pack frame and backpack sat next to me on the ground. I pulled out my black sketchbook and opened it to the back page. The graphic artist in me had written in black letters: TUCS, as there wasn't enough space for the whole word. I held it up to cars that passed by, figuring the sign would be more informative than my thumb. There I stood, a human road sign. Three-thousand miles of highway lay ahead of me. Excitement had replaced nervousness as I waited for my journey to begin, hopeful my first ride would appear at any moment.

I waited.... And I waited....

During the next hour, the occasional cars passed without stopping. I realized waiting—perhaps hours—between rides would likely repeat over and over again until I finally reached my destination. I had no control over my timetable. As I waited, it gave time to reconsider my scheme. In the back of my mind, a gnawing little voice suggested I walk to a phone booth and call Kate to pick me up. The voice grew louder and more insistent with each vehicle that ignored me. "This might not be such a good idea," I said quietly, watching a station wagon pass me by, heading west.

Suddenly a large motorhome approached and slowed down, then actually pulled over and stopped. Lost in doubtful thought, I couldn't believe someone had stopped to pick me up until the door swung open. The sounds of contemporary rock music flowed out the door. A pleasant-looking man in his forties smiled at me. "Come aboard," he said, motioning me in with a friendly gesture. "Goin' to Tucson?"

"Yes." I climbed in.

"Too bad."

"Why?"

"I'm leaving for Denver in two days. I could have taken you most of the way."

For a moment, I considered that maybe I should wait a couple of days and take advantage of the offer but quickly dismissed the idea, afraid I'd never leave. "Well, at least you're getting me started, so I appreciate the ride." As the driver closed the door, doubt transformed into excitement at my first ride. I was finally on my way.

From the passenger seat, I looked around the motorhome's well-appointed interior, tempted briefly to wait and travel in style more than halfway to Tucson. I gave up that thought as the road lay ahead, framed by the huge windshield, giving my official start a widescreen cinematic feeling for the drama to come. The man threw the motorhome into gear, and we took to the road under a clear blue sky, and I smiled. Naked trees slipped past the big windows as a new song played on the radio. But when the refrain began, the smile faded, and the words pierced my mind and soul: "*Pain will come back to you. Pain will come back to you...*" I couldn't help feeling the song was some sort of dark omen.

The feeling passed when the song ended, and we cruised down a long slope towards the Connecticut River. Tall green pine trees and dormant hardwoods lined the road, waiting for spring as we made for Brattleboro, Vermont.

"Why are you going to Tucson?" he asked. I explained, and then he shook his head in disbelief. Naturally, his next question was, "How'd you ever convince your wife to let you go?"

"Maybe she's as crazy as I am."

We reached Brattleboro and approached I-91. He stopped by the southbound entrance ramp, and I climbed out. "Thanks for the ride."

"Good luck, and have a safe trip." He waved goodbye and drove off.

Encouraged that I'd reached my first milestone, I assumed the posture, pack sitting next to me, sign in hand before my chest. But it was a dead place to stand. During half an hour, I watched a dozen cars enter the highway. Trying not to get discouraged, I patiently waited. At least the sun felt warm.

Finally, a pair of thirty-something, scruffy-looking guys stopped. I got in the back of their beat-up four-door sedan that smelled of pot, and we headed south. They were going to Greenfield, Massachusetts, a little over twenty miles away. There was minimal conversation until the passenger turned around with a wide grin. "Hey man, want a hit?" He offered me a crooked joint, which I accepted to help make my journey more enjoyable.

I was feeling pretty good when they dropped me off at the Greenfield exit. I walked to the entrance ramp, snacked on the sandwich Kate had sent me off with, and waited. A couple of cars passed me as they turned onto the ramp. With each vehicle, it was difficult not to get disheartened at being ignored. From where I stood, I saw a much greater volume of traffic heading south on the Interstate. *This is bullshit*, I thought. Emboldened by necessity or numbed by the pot, I decided to risk walking up to the highway and try my luck there. I knew the cops would be less apt to bother me on the entrance ramp than standing directly on the road, but all those potential cars driving south was a compelling reason to take the risk.

Just as I started walking, a dark blue Volkswagen Bug pulled alongside and waved me in. I put my bag in the back seat and sat down. The driver was a young man about my age, wearing an L.L. Bean jacket and jeans. His close-cropped hair was blonde, and he had pale blue eyes set in a pleasant face. "My name's Judd. I'm going to Englewood, New Jersey."

I was stunned. "That's great!" It wasn't quite eleven o'clock, and I had a solid ride that would take me about 180 miles. *I'll be across the Hudson River around three this afternoon. My third ride will put me just west of New York City.* I introduced myself as we entered the highway. Judd shifted through the gears, accompanied by the characteristic sounds of the Volkswagen air-cooled engine.

Judd was pleasant and talkative. He spoke of his girlfriend then complained that his parents didn't care much for her. He then went on to complain about how much his parents annoyed him.

"What sort of work do you do?" I asked.

"I don't."

"Between jobs?"

"No. I don't have to work. My father's a stockbroker and gives me what I want. What about you?"

As I told him about myself, he observed me like a bug or alien species. My poverty was utterly out of his scope. Telling him I was married with soon to be five children was more than he could imagine.

"How can you handle so many kids?"

I laughed and then said, "It's never dull."

"What possessed you? At your age, taking on kids?"

"I really wanted a family. I came from a reasonable home and wanted to share what I experienced."

Judd shook his head, trying to process what he heard. We drove in silence as we crossed the Connecticut River at Springfield, then back over it again before Hartford, Connecticut.

"So, if you're married, your wife's pregnant, and there're four kids in the house, why are you going to Tucson? Sounds like you're running away from your family."

"That's what my father-in-law thinks." I gazed out the window feeling a cloud of doubt shadow my mind.

Judd looked at me. "Are you?"

"Abandoning my family never occurred to me." Doubt evaporated. "I'm doing this because I love them. I have to change my life for their sake."

"So, did you wake up one morning and say, I gotta go to Tucson?"

"Shoes."

"Shoes?"

"The idea came to me because of shoes the other morning." I began to explain my journey as we turned onto I-84 west at Hartford. I told him about our money struggles, my background as a college dropout, and a struggling commercial artist.

"Sounds rough," Judd interjected. "What do you expect to find?"

"Find?" I hadn't thought that I'd find anything. I was going to think of a plan.

Judd stuck out his lower lip and nodded. "Sounds to me like a vision quest."

"What's that?"

He raised his eyebrows, surprised that I was unaware of the term. "Didn't you say you lived in a hippy commune? Don't they all have teepees and a bunch of Indian paraphernalia?"

"There was only one guy who seemed to be into the Indian stuff. He was a forty-year-old Jew from Brooklyn who sported a pair of wiry braids. The only spiritual thing he was into was American Spirit cigarettes. The guy told me if he said a prayer to the spirits with each cigarette, he'd never get cancer."

Judd shook his head. "Well, a vision quest is a thing some American Indians do. Kind of a supernatural practice when someone gets in touch with their guardian spirit, usually an animal spirit that offers advice to the seeker."

"You mean I'm supposed to find a wolf or a bear or something and ask for career advice?" I chuckled.

“Maybe,” Judd responded. “That’s the point of the quest. When they begin, they don’t know where it will take them or what form the guardian spirit will take.”

“I don’t know. Sounds weird.”

Judd laughed. “You’re already knee-deep into weird. Look at you. It’s pretty damn weird that you left your wife and family to hitchhike across the country.”

I nodded slowly. “You got me there.”

“Sounds like you got a real problem on your hands, so you’re going on a quest to find yourself.” He glanced at me. “Okay, skip the Indian mumbo-jumbo. Think about some of the old prophets. Look at Moses—”

“Moses? I’m no prophet. I’m just some guy who’s scared that I can’t support my wife and family—”

“I’m not suggesting you’re a prophet. That’s not the point.”

“Then, why bring up Moses?”

“That man was on a quest. He was fat and happy as a Prince of Egypt until he finds out he’s a Jew. He starts asking questions, pisses off Pharaoh, and gets exiled to the desert. While he’s in the desert, living in hardship, fasting, no water, getting baked under the sun, it all transformed him. He even thought he talked to God, who then told him what to do.” Judd grinned and tapped his temple with an index finger. “He came up with a plan.”

Judd’s words required some thought. I gazed out the window as the VW struggled to climb a long grade ahead of Waterbury. Finally, “I think I see what you’re driving at. Getting away, struggling, and coming up with a plan.” I grinned. “Who knows? Maybe I’ll find my guardian spirit, and it’ll tell me what to do.”

“Well, at least you’ll escape the madness for a while.”

“Yes. That’s the point.” Suddenly, I realized it fit with Judd’s vision quest and Moses’ story. “I guess, living amidst the chaos and financial pressure, I couldn’t possibly do what is required.”

"Who could think straight in that confusion?"

"Certainly, the distractions of survival, daily life, and worry fully occupy my mind."

"See?" Judd tapped the steering wheel. "You're literally going to the desert and need to purge all of that shit."

"I need to get away from everything that distracts me so I can get clarity and sort out my life." Judd was the first person I'd talked to at this level other than Kate. My journey began to make sense in that context.

"Well, hitchhiking's a risky business," he added. "I wish you the best of luck."

Time quickly passed as we talked. We turned south on I-684 at Brewster, New York. Not only had we covered miles, but as we drove further south, we were advancing in time. The weather was generally warmer, and spring was closer at hand based on trees with swollen buds about to burst with new leaves. Traffic was light as we crossed the Tappan Zee Bridge over the Hudson just north of New York City. We drove down the Palisades Parkway into New Jersey and would soon be in Englewood.

"How 'bout we go to my house? You can have something to eat before I take you over to I-80." I was grateful for the suggestion. Having a good meal before I tried to get a ride toward Pennsylvania sounded like a great idea.

We drove down a few streets lined with large, expensive homes and eventually pulled into one that seemed opulent even for that neighborhood. Obviously, Judd's father was a successful stockbroker. I expected servants and all, but we were the only people in the house. I was thrilled by the array of food Judd set before me in the enormous, well-appointed kitchen. We ate and talked about nothing in particular.

When Judd finished eating, he stood and took his plate to the sink. "Make yourself a couple of sandwiches and take something else for later on," he insisted. After I stocked my larder, it was getting late, and Judd sensed I was anxious to get going. He drove me over to the highway and dropped me off at an entrance ramp to I-80 west.

I got out and set my pack down to get my sign. Judd got out of the VW and handed me a piece of paper. "Here's my phone number. If you can, give me a call and let me know how it all works out."

I shook his hand and thanked him for the ride and the food. He got back in his car, waved goodbye, and headed home. It was now about four o'clock, and the sun was getting low on the horizon. Though it was warmer than home, it was still cold and getting colder as the afternoon waned. After being in New Hampshire for several years, the urban crowding was an unusual experience. However, I took comfort in the higher traffic volume, hoping it would improve my odds for another ride.

My luck seemed to be holding. Within ten minutes, an old green Chevy station wagon pulled over and let me in. A man named Fred greeted me and said he was on his way to Hazleton, Pennsylvania. *I'm moving right along*. That ride would take me another 130 miles further west to the junction of I-81 south and warmer weather.

Fred asked about my destination, and I explained my situation and purpose. He reacted with surprise and whistled in disbelief. When I got around to telling him I was a commercial artist, he said, "I'm not an artist, but I'm an artist's model."

"Really?"

"I'm a friend of the Brother's Hildebrandt." I knew they were popular artists who illustrated posters and calendars for Tolkien's *Lord of the Rings* series. He laughed and said, "Do you recognize me?"

I was familiar with their work, so I looked at the large burly man with thick wavy hair but couldn't place his character.

He laughed again, "I'm Gimley, the dwarf." Fred smiled at me. "Do *I* look like a dwarf?"

"I suppose if I just look at your face."

We covered the width of New Jersey and crossed over the Delaware River into Pennsylvania. Night settled in as we climbed into the Allegheny

Mountains. The lack of lights and fewer exits—many with no services—were signs of a sparse population density, much like New Hampshire. I gazed into the darkness beyond the cones of light cast by his headlights and observed that traffic was pretty light. When we reached I-81, we turned south and climbed up the long grade to Hazleton. I knew it was a sizable community, which gave me hope for better opportunities for a ride. We passed the first Hazleton exit, brightly lit with a hotel and gas station. We passed another exit, and when he finally got off the highway, stopped at the bottom of the ramp. Fred wished me luck and a successful journey. It was now about 7:00 p.m.

Chapter 4

Reality

AFTER HIS STATION WAGON DROVE AWAY, TWO THINGS STRUCK ME. First, it was dark and cold. Hazleton was at a higher elevation, so the temperature was more like Marlow. As I stood there, shivering, the second reality became very clear. I was in a very isolated spot with no gas station or any kind of store or place to eat. Just a bridge that crossed the highway and my entrance ramp. No lights, no cars, no people, or even houses to be seen. At that moment, reality sank home, and the refrain of the song crept back into my head, "*Pain will come back to you.*"

Daylight was long gone. It would be ten hours before the sun ignited the first flicker of dawn. During my mental preparation for the journey, I neglected to consider hitchhiking at night, let alone during increasingly cold, windy, and cloudy weather. There was no traffic on the road where I stood or on the highway below.

I kept looking at my watch, but the dimly glowing and barely visible hands seemed as frozen as the air. After about forty minutes, my shivering took on a dark quality. Fear crept into my mind as the refrain repeated. Another hour passed, and despair joined the noisy party in my head. An hour later, I counted the fifth car that passed me on the lonely road. My morbid count of the traffic passing on the Interstate below was equally grim. Twenty vehicles in all drove through the night, split evenly between the north and southbound lanes, most of it tractor-trailer trucks. If I stood on the highway, I'd risk a greater chance of attracting the police's unwanted attention. Yet, if I stayed where I was, it could be all night before anyone even turned onto my entrance ramp. I decided to chance going down the ramp and try my luck on the highway.

I hoisted my pack and walked. Moving warmed me slightly, but even though accustomed to the low temperatures, my teeth chattered. I reached the point where the ramp merged onto the highway and watched a dribble of traffic speed past me. Tractor-trailers looked huge and scary as they blew by, physically shaking my body with the wall of cold air pushed ahead of the massive vehicles, their engines then fading in the distance, followed by an eerie silence.

I stood in the pitch black, my ears straining for the sound of any approaching vehicle. When I detected an engine sound slowly growing louder, hope rose with the noise. Finally, in the distance, headlights would rise like twin moons that approached with painful slowness, my body pulled toward them like the tide. Hope built to a crescendo until it burst when the white lights flashed past. Turning in disappointment, I watched the red taillights shrink and disappear around a curve some five-hundred yards away. A few moments later, once again, I stood in the silent empty night—waiting. Bored and hungry, I finished off the last of my food from Judd's house.

My watch was a curse and a blessing. Minutes ticked slowly by, as the second hand dimly swept around, which provided scant companionship and comfort. But the watch also made me painfully aware of just how much time had passed. When I saw the face in rare passing headlights, I moaned. It was after 2:05 a.m. I nervously walked back and forth, calling out, "God, bring me a car. Please bring me a ride."

I felt awfully sorry for myself, giving little thought that I'd created the situation. My family was back in Marlow, tucked in warm beds, while "Bozo" Dad stood freezing his ass off in the middle of nowhere. *What was I thinking?* At that moment, there was a stark contrast between standing in empty icy blackness and the overcrowded, noisy house with no place to think. "*Pain will come back to you,*" continued with greater frequency than passing cars. The song said it all. It appeared that I got immediate payback for leaving Kate with the kids as I ran off on some crazy selfish trip.

I waited, begging aloud for a car to just drive by and show me some headlights. I stomped numb feet and rubbed frozen fingers. Then I heard an unusual noise.

It was faint but slowly grew louder. *A bad muffler?* I thought. *No. More like some coughing and struggling car.* A glow appeared behind the hill's crest, heralding the first car to pass in half an hour. I froze, anticipating the rising headlights. The sound grew louder. Then two bright dots crested the hill. I held up the sign high over my head, long before the driver could see me. "Please stop. Please stop," I pleaded.

I watched the lights come closer, or was it my mind playing tricks? *Is he slowing down? Yes. I'm sure he's slowing. Oh, God!* "Don't get on the exit ramp. Please don't," I implored quietly. Then the underside of the bridge lit up, indicating he was still approaching. I throttled my hopes to reduce the likely disappointment. Suddenly, a yellow turn signal rhythmically winked at me. The vehicle slowed, and then it stopped practically at my feet. The engine sputtered and coughed. I stood there, wondering if it was some strange mirage until I finally picked up my pack and approached the car rattling as it struggled to idle.

Chapter 5

Sundance

A LIGHT CAME ON INSIDE THE VEHICLE, where a man who looked about thirty-five waved me to come toward him. I opened the door, suddenly greeted with the thick odor of cigarette smoke. "You want a ride or not?" he sounded impatient.

"Sure do." I tossed my pack in the back seat then flopped into the beat-up old Rambler sedan. I pulled the squeaky door shut with a thud as the driver pressed the accelerator. The engine made a funny rumbling sound, and after a lurching start, we slowly moved onto the highway.

I looked at my watch. "Man, I'm glad you picked me up."

"Been there long?"

"I've been standing out there for about seven hours." It felt wonderful to be off my feet and sitting in a warm, moving car again. As I relaxed into the worn seat, I regarded my benefactor.

He was a classic hippy about ten years past his expiration date. A brown ponytail of indeterminate length disappeared between his back and the seat. The long wiry matching beard hung from his chin, dusting his chest. The full mustache drooped like a tattered awning, hiding the mouth from which a glowing cigarette poked through the facial hair. He blew a plume of smoke over gnarled hands clutching the steering wheel, which wiggled back and forth, making the vehicle feel dangerously unstable. I couldn't tell if his hands or worn ball joints caused the car's shimmy. He removed the cigarette butt, tossed it out the window, then reached into a large grocery bag between us and grabbed a handful of cashews. Somehow, he found and filled the hole beneath the frazzled hair. "Wanph phum?" he pointed at the bag. I gladly accepted and filled my mouth with the salty nuts.

I waited for him to speak first. Eventually, he introduced himself, "I'm Sundance." As he piloted the rattletrap down the empty road at seventy miles an hour, he said, "I was falling asleep and needed some company to keep me awake."

"Glad to oblige. I was desperate for a ride, and I'm happy to keep you awake."

Sundance was eager to report his mission. "I left Albany this afternoon and got to get to Newport, Tennessee."

"How come?"

Suddenly, he exploded into a torrent of expletives and cusswords that turned the inside of the car blue. "My goddamn wife, Sunflower, ran off with our ten-year-old daughter, Venus. Woke up this morning, and they were gone. Just a fuckin' note on the fridge that said, *Gone to Mother's*. Bullshit! Goin' to her mother's house in Newport. Shit!" The enraged driver violently wrestled with the shaking wheel. "That goddamn Richard's down there. I know what the fuck those two cooked up. You should've seen that son of a bitch last Christmas lookin' at Sunflower. Couldn't keep his dirty paws off her." Sundance was beside himself. I must have been the first person he got to vent his anger at since he woke up that morning. "That damn bitch took the fuckin' pickup. Hell, I just tuned it up and changed the oil last week. She left me with this piece a shit." He banged his fist on the wiggling wheel. "She thought it wasn't running. Fuck her, man! She made me so goddamn mad. I'll show her. Took me all morning to get this shit box to run."

Run? I thought as I listened to the rough engine and felt the violently shaking car as he pushed toward eighty. *How the hell did he get this far? We'll be lucky to reach Virginia—*

“That bitch thought she’d get away from me. Crap! Took my daughter. Took my fuckin’ truck!” Another bash on the wheel. “Fuck her! When I catch up with her, she’s gonna be fuckin’ sorry.” It seemed what pissed him off most was that she took the better vehicle and left him with the crappy Rambler. He kept complaining about all the work he did to fix it and held up his right hand. “Look at these knuckles. All bashed to shit fuckin’ with those goddamn bolts!”

Sundance looked like he was grinning under his facial hair, but I couldn’t tell in the dim light. “I’ll fix her just like I fixed this pile a shit.” He balled his hand into a fist, “Maybe I’ll bloody my fuckin’ knuckles on her face.” I squirmed uncomfortably, fearing I’d been picked up by a psycho driving a deathtrap. I seriously considered how I might bailout from a moving vehicle.

Sundance told me when he got the Rambler running, he picked up the bag of cashews, a couple of six-packs of coke, and hit the road ready for a fight. “I’ll kick that asshole Richard’s fuckin’ ass back to Georgia, where he fuckin’ belongs.” He leaned over the wheel; shoulders tensed like a boxer about to explode from his corner. “Then, I’ll dump this piece of shit and drag Sunflower and Venus back in the pickup.”

I was struck by his warped yet perhaps misplaced devotion to his wife and child. It was strange driving through the night with another husband and father, who appeared to care so much for his family he couldn’t let them go—couldn’t let his wife separate him from his daughter. I couldn’t judge whether Sundance or Sunflower was the better parent. But this guy was enraged at the thought of someone splitting up his family, willing to drive hundreds of miles to fight for them. But, like some sort of captive therapist, I listened as he went on and on for miles and miles, well after sunrise. Over and over, he repeated the same thing. He only stopped ranting when he lit a cigarette, stuff cashews in his mouth, drink soda, or stop putting gas in the tank and oil in the crankcase. Slugging down Coke after Coke, we rattled and shook at highspeed toward Newport, nearly six-hundred miles away.

Ranting, cigarettes, cashews, Coke. It was an endless cycle as we made our way through Maryland and down the Shenandoah Valley in western Virginia. Despite his incessant tirade—which now had become little more than white noise—I drifted off to sleep for a couple of hours, waking up in southern Virginia, where I-81 climbed up and down long hills. I don't know how he did it, but he kept blathering about Sunflower, Richard, and the mayhem they could expect. If anything, his energy grew more violent the closer we got to Newport.

I turned away, looking out the window as we drove past trees now covered with new leaves, past white flowering Bartlett pears, and bright pink redbuds. By the time we reached Tennessee, Spring was in full bloom.

Sundance and I would part company when we reached I-40 westbound, and I'd begin the long-haul to the desert southwest. During the ten-hour drive from Hazleton, I had barely spoken. All he knew was my name and that I was from New Hampshire. By the time he stopped the car, Sundance had cranked himself into a murderous rage. He was within a half-hour of his mother-in-law's house and the likely violent showdown with Richard and Sunflower.

I scrambled out of the decrepit Rambler to the safety of the roadside, glad to be alive, glad I wasn't Richard. I waved goodbye, but Sundance didn't notice as he pulled away, clattering down the road, trailing a plume of blue exhaust. As I watched the Rambler smoke and diminished in the distance, I realized we shared a brief, yet strange fellowship, two parents on a quest to save our families. I shuddered, considering his violent intentions, and wondered what would happen when he burst into his mother-in-law's house, and the players collided like two masses of enriched Plutonium.

When Sundance disappeared, I was ready to continue my quest, glad that it was a financial problem and not the triangle that faced that troubled man. Regardless of my concerns, I was grateful for the long ride that had gotten me as far as Tennessee. I figured listening to him complain the whole distance was a small price to pay for the ride and the peculiar entertainment derived from a madman's rantings.

Chapter 6

Tennessee

THE AIR WAS GLORIOUSLY WARM UNDER THE BRIGHT NOONDAY SUN. I knew then the southern route was the right choice. After such a long ride, it was a relief that Sundance dropped me off at an entrance ramp with a gas station and small store. I got something to eat other than cashews and Coke and then took advantage of their bathroom, washed my face, and headed to the entrance ramp.

I was excited to be about six-hundred miles farther south and begin the long stretch across the American heartland. This route was familiar. I knew what it was like to drive the vast expanse of the central plains and on into the Rocky Mountains, but hitchhiking was turning out to be something else. When you're driving, you can come and go as you please, but now I was at the mercy of other drivers. I hoped someone who needed the company for a long-distance drive would pick me up. "I'm lucky the weather's so pleasant," I remarked to myself, gazing skyward and then wondered about the weather back home. Spring, with its new leaves and green grass, was weeks away from Marlow, and weeks before Kate and the kids could be outside without winter clothing. As I enjoyed the warmth on my face, I felt a stab of guilt but quickly pushed it away. "I was freezing my ass off last night. I'm going to enjoy the good weather."

My next milestone would be crossing the Mississippi River at Memphis. I knew it was about five-hundred miles—a seven-hour trip if I was driving. But I wasn't, and it was nearly an hour before I got a thirty-mile ride that dropped me off in the middle of nowhere. There I waited another hour to travel fifty miles, depositing me once again in rural central. Because there was no traffic on the empty county road, I had to wait on the highway if I had any hope for a ride. Sweat slid down my back as I heated under the sun, and the pleasant novelty of warm weather quickly wore off and happened to look at my feet. *Damn shoes are responsible for dumping me in rural Tennessee*. My head shook. *No, that's wrong thinking. I'm supposed to be figuring out a miraculous new career. Haven't thought about that since before I left*— Suddenly, a tractor-trailer roared by, pushing a wall of air that brushed me back from the road and pushed new career thoughts right out of my mind. My attention returned to get the next ride. *Hell, I've got plenty of time to think of something.*

I waited for a half-hour before a car stopped just past me. Excited, I approached the dark brown Chevy Impala but stopped short to discover a Tennessee State trooper wearing his nicely starched uniform sitting in the unmarked car. I was surprised that this was my first encounter with the law. He rolled down the window and politely explained, "Y'all can't hitchhak own an Interstate hahway. Y'all have to go back down the entrance ramp and wait there."

I knew exactly what to do. "Yes, sir." I was very polite, turned around, and started walking. Long ago, following various encounters with the law, I'd learned that respecting the police was the surest way to avoid unnecessary trouble. When I looked back, he was watching me in the rearview mirror. I trudged back down the ramp to the deserted road before he pulled away. I waited for another hour, and not a single vehicle passed. By now, it was around three o'clock, and night would soon be upon me. The thought of standing alone through another night in such a rural location was distressing. I decided to take my chances and walk back up the ramp to hold up my sign where passing traffic could actually see me.

I waited another forty minutes, then a loud red pickup truck approached, with two guys sitting in the cab who looked my age, wearing ball caps cocked on the back of their heads. They slowed, pulled over, and stopped about fifty yards away. A big Confederate flag hung in the back window of the truck. Suddenly, waving arms sprouted from either side. Thrilled for a ride, I slung my pack over one shoulder and ran toward the pickup. Just as I reached the tailgate, the rear tires suddenly spun wildly, showering me with sand and gravel as the truck sped away with a throaty roar. The horn honked as arms once again emerged from both sides, this time flipping me the bird. "Damn you!" I shouted. I'd been the victim of the classic fifty-yard drill. "So much for southern hospitality."

Around four o'clock, I got a ride from a pleasant older couple who drove me just past Nashville, which put me more than halfway to Memphis. It was now dark and after seven o'clock as I waited once again. "*Pain will come back to you*," crept back into my consciousness as I stood in the dark, hoping I wouldn't meet up with another cop or some more southern rednecks. Within fifteen minutes, another pickup stopped, and an older man in his fifties waved me in.

"Ma name's Carl. Ahm goin' to Memphis."

"Thanks for the ride!"

Unlike my drive with Sundance, Carl was calm and happy. He was a skinny guy with a weathered face and graying hair slicked back on his square head, wearing a long-sleeved dark blue mechanics shirt and dirty bib overalls. When I told him my mission, he nodded his head slowly. "Damn! Y'all must be sum kinda sweet talker."

For the next three hours, it was mindless conversation, though I did learn one piece of interesting information from Carl. "Ah got ma own private coal mine. It's just a cut in the side a ma hill. Me an ma brother work it alone. We got one bi-yer fur 'r coal. Kin you guess who that customer is?" he grinned like an excited kid.

"I have no clue."

"Kingsford!" he said like I should know what he meant.

"What?"

"Kingsford bahs 'r coal to make 'em li'l charcoal breequettes."

"Coal?"

"Yep. They grind 'r coal enta dust. Mix it with corn starch an small flecks ah wood charcoal. They gots a big machine that cumpresses the mixture to make them li'l grillin' breequettes."

"Imagine that." I was genuinely surprised.

When he let me off in East Memphis, it was after 10:00 p.m.

It wasn't as desolate as some of my stops, but there was very little traffic at that time of night. Off to the west, Memphis cast a dull red glow on the underside of clouds. Low clouds that had rolled in all afternoon. *I'm close to the river, but it looks like a change in the weather.*

After nearly an hour, a small yellow Toyota sedan pulled up. Much to my surprise, sitting in the front were two women who looked about thirty. *Are they nuts?* I wondered about the judgment and sanity of two females picking up a strange guy on the side of the road in the middle of the night.

"Get in," said the passenger.

"Sure," I pushed my pack in first and climbed in the back seat. The odor of strong perfume filled my nostrils.

"You got a long way to go?" giggled the driver.

"Yup. And thanks to you ladies, I'll be a little closer." I leaned back in the seat. "How far do you go?"

They burst out laughing at my innocent but loaded question. "Not as far as you'd like, sweetie." I suspected the two women might have been a bit drunk. The passenger, an attractive brunette, rested her arm on the seat and turned to me. She dropped her head on the crooked arm and giggled.

"Don't mahnd Cindy," said the driver, trying to control her laughter as well as the car. "It's late, and we're goin' home from a party. We live in Memphis, so that's as far as we go tonight, honey."

When Cindy stopped laughing, she asked, "Wadder you doin' out here?"

I explained my trip to the heavily lidded passenger, whose head lolled on her arm, trying to focus on me. Curious about why I was on the road, they asked me to explain.

When I finished, the driver said, "No way ah'd let ma husband leave me alone while I was cookin' a baby and mindin' yo kids. Is she some kinda nut?"

"I think we both are," was all I could manage.

We made our way into Memphis along I-40, which turns south into downtown. By then, it was pushing midnight, and the only traffic was a few occasional tractor-trailers. The city had that late-night glow of streetlights and empty buildings lit up for decoration and to discourage intruders. The driver swerved toward her exit ramp and stopped too quickly, jolting me into the back of the passenger seat. "End of the line, sweetie," she announced as Cindy giggled.

"Thanks for the ride, ladies," I said, climbing out of the Toyota. When I shut the door, the car sped away and swept down the arcing exit ramp and out of sight.

I stood along an empty highway the previous night with nothing around me—dark and cold. At least I was warm, but this was a different sort of nowhere. The Interstate ran through a deserted downtown, surrounded by empty buildings and very little traffic. Despite the urban setting, I wasn't having any better luck getting a ride, but I felt just as alone and even more vulnerable than I was in Hazelton.

Finally, around one a.m., I'd had enough and began walking. I thought I'd walk until someone picked me up but hoped it wouldn't be a local cop looking to hassle me. I kept walking. Only tractor-trailers rumbled past, buffeting me as they pushed through the night air.

After a couple of miles, I'd walked myself into a problem.

Chapter 7

The Crossing

DIRECTLY IN FRONT OF ME, LARGE GREEN SIGNS MADE IT CLEAR WHAT LAY AHEAD. The highway had slowly climbed above the surrounding buildings and streets. The steep grassy embankment had given way to an elevated road set on concrete piers, and I was now thirty feet above empty parking lots and industrial structures. At the same time, the shoulder had grown narrower. I turned my head back toward Memphis, which looked much smaller beneath the reddish clouds. I'd walked a couple of miles from downtown without seeing a single car, nothing but big rigs heading back and forth above the Mississippi River. I set my pack down and rubbed aching shoulders. It was time to stop and consider the situation.

I was at the point of no return and had to make a decision. "Either I turn around and head back toward the city and … And do what?" Dawn was hours away, and traffic wouldn't pick up until six or seven. I had no place to go if I went back, except to a police station, because I was sure a cop had to drive by sooner or later and remove me from the highway. Even if I avoided the police, I'd have to find someplace to wait that wasn't on the Interstate, which was at the last exit I passed a half-mile back. "Who knows if it'll be any better in the daylight?" These were not comforting thoughts. A tractor-trailer blew past; the wall of air pushed me like a stiff arm. My eyes followed it, heading west.

Beyond the large signs over the road, the superstructure rose in the distance, outlined with bright points of light. It was bad enough where I stood because there wasn't much room for anyone to get off the road to stop and pick me up. I saw ahead that the shoulder all but disappeared. "If I take one more step west, I can't turn back." I kept talking to myself, hoping I'd answer. "Once I start, I can't stop 'til I'm off the bridge, across the river into Arkansas." My feet refused to do anything as my mind weighed the options. Neither one was appealing, and both had their dangers. However, the thought of backtracking was appalling.

On the other hand, walking across the Mississippi River was oddly appealing. It presented a once in a lifetime opportunity. "After all, if I just walk and don't stop, it shouldn't be dangerous." My voice sounded mildly assuring, so I hoisted the pack onto my shoulders, adjusted its weight, and headed west.

Talk about the audacity of youth affecting my judgment. I suppose it's easy, with hindsight in my favor, to say I should have done anything to avoid walking across that damn bridge. But I hadn't a clue and didn't even attempt to consider the reality of my decision. Other than the highway maintenance crew—who had the benefit of safety cones keeping traffic away—I doubt many people have actually walked the length of that bridge.

I crossed a shorter span then began the approach to the main bridge. Slowly the first steel arch rose ahead of me. I was about to walk over the Mississippi River. There was no stopping now. No one other than the cops would stop for me on the bridge. I rose with the highway over the empty streets below. The steel girders of the arch curved upward, outlined in twinkling lights.

I'd driven over that bridge before. It was close to two miles from where I stood to the opposite end, but driving is different. At sixty miles an hour, it takes about two minutes to cross; vertical support cables and guard railing flicker past, breaking up the view of the broad river below. Then the highway drops back down, and the river is gone. Just another geographical feature is made inconsequential by motor vehicles and Interstate Highway.

On foot, the crossing was an entirely different experience, especially in the early morning darkness. It was a formidable distance over the black water and would take close to an hour to cross on foot. When I drove over the bridge, it didn't matter that the guardrail was a short lip of concrete topped with a ribbon of steel railing with posts just three feet tall. My feet barely fit between the solid white line separating the traffic and the thigh-high railing. I was top-heavy and unstable, with the big backpack sitting high on my shoulders.

A large green sign with *Mississippi River* in white letters hung above as I entered the steel lattice of the first arch. Next to me, the lower girders of the supporting arch began to curve upward. At a slow and careful walking speed, nothing flickered past. I moved like a snail creeping to safety, seeming to get nowhere fast.

Streetlights cast pools of light on the gray concrete road surface, and the dashed white lines that appeared much longer on foot vanished into perspective. Arching metal swept higher, and every fifty feet, a light burned at each riveted junction of girders and plate steel. Progressively longer suspension cables, the size of my forearm, hung beneath each lamp. I thought them impossibly thin strands incapable of supporting the concrete and steel bridge deck's massive weight. The bad feeling amplified when trucks rumbled past, and I felt the bridge sag under the heavy vehicles. It was unnerving to walk on the noticeably undulating structure as it climbed higher over the invisible surface below. As the wind gusted down the river and the wall of air pushed by each truck shook my body, I felt unstable and vulnerable. With each buffeting blast of air, my stomach knotted, and I tried not to look over the side. The guardrail was too low to hold onto, and due to my high center of gravity, I feared any moment a passing truck would knock me off balance, sending me over the side to the river far below.

One foot after another, I walked, focusing on the far side of the bridge. It seemed to take forever, but eventually, the graceful steel arch curved back down to the bridge deck. Ahead hung a large sign with *Arkansas* boldly proclaiming the state boundary. Small comfort as I wasn't even halfway across the river. To reach the safety of the other side, I had to cross beneath another identical arch that rose before me. Next to the worthless guardrail, I kept walking along the narrow shoulder, passing each suspension cable, looking up at girders curving far overhead. Beneath my feet, the flexing bridge felt less unnerving, but I still feared getting knocked over the side or meeting a cop who might feel obligated to pull me in for the night.

A huge truck in the lane next to the shoulder approached from behind. I looked back, blinded by rapidly closing headlights. Instinctively, I moved away, my thigh pressing against the cold metal guardrail, my upper body caught by the forceful wall of air pushed by the square truck cab. I crouched, reached for the low guardrail, grasping the metal, convinced I'd left indentations from my fingers. I froze in place as the trailer swept past. My knees weakened, and I shook as I looked down into the blackness. I didn't want to move but knew I must get off the bridge before another truck brushed me over the side. "Move!" I scolded myself to get going. At first, slowly, still unsure of my balance, I picked up the pace to end the ordeal.

I wondered what would have happened if I fell. *I doubt I'd survive the fall, but if I did, I'd surely drown in the middle of the river*. I thought of Kate and the kids, realizing my being dead would be a bigger problem than being broke. *Is this trip worth it? Is it worth risking my life to better my family? I must be kidding myself. How can I possibly come up with any sort of realistic career plan?* Fear replaced guilt; doubt replaced fear. One foot after the other, I moved. I struggled with the concept of being away from my family, searching for what I didn't know I might or might not discover. "Judd was right," I spoke aloud to hear a human voice. "The stress of the journey's working on my mind, starting to strip away the bullshit." With each step, I worked to suppress unproductive feelings. "I've come this far; I'm not going to turn around and head home." The prospects of crossing back over the bridge propelled me forward. Thinking of the men before me struggling to reach distant goldfields bolstered me. It was a question of risk vs. reward. I was gambling that the risk I exposed myself to, tested in the crucible of my quest, would reveal the reward in a plan for our financial salvation.

Eventually, the second arch descended, and I knew the other side of the river was near. But even when I emerged beneath the steel framework and the unobstructed dim sky spread above, I still had a long walk before reaching the end of the western bridge approach. Ahead of me, alternating from one side to the other, streetlights atop tall poles arched over and lit the road's diminishing perspective. Behind me, the lights of Memphis faded as dawn cast a dull rosy glow on the cloudy eastern sky.

The bridge approach imperceptibly lowered to the broad floodplain of the Mississippi. Finally, the narrow shoulder gave way to the standard width and a grassy bank, sloping down from the highway. Arkansas slowly emerged from the gray dawn, which revealed a flat horizon, broken with clumps of large hardwood trees.

I made it! I felt like the chicken that crossed the road. I got to the other side and survived the passage. The previous night I felt alone and helpless, desperate for a ride. This night I didn't wait. I pushed myself on foot to cross one of the significant barriers on the planet. Not walking on water, but precariously above, on the well-engineered Hernando DeSoto Bridge. I accomplished something, and despite being tired and exhausted, I felt proud and excited.

Walking along the deserted highway, I saw the Mississippi's west bank stretched out as a broad flat plain surrounding me. It was light now, but low gray scud clouds passed overhead, releasing their moisture, coating my face with wet mist. When I finally reached the first exit, it was discouraging to find nothing there, so I continued on another couple of miles to the next one. I was relieved to see a gas station, a diner, and a convenience store where I could get food and a needed break.

Chapter 8

Faith

IT WAS ABOUT 8:30 A.M. AND MY THIRD DAY ON THE ROAD. Any glamour about hitching was long gone, especially as heavily laden clouds descended. The fine mist soon became a steady rain. I couldn't expect clear weather during my journey to Tucson, but having walked across the bridge, I hated standing in the rain. After an hour, I was discouraged enough to think about going back to the store and get out of the shower until it stopped. But without knowing how long it would last, I decided to stay and hold up my sign, silently pleading to God for one of the passing vehicles to give me a ride.

A short while later, a big old white Chevy Impala stopped with the passenger door right in front of me. I leaned over to see a smiling man waving me into his vehicle. I opened the door. "Thanks for the ride. You're a Godsend." I settled into the seat. The heavyset driver grinned. He looked to be in his fifties, with almost black hair combed neatly to one side. Set in his round face were pale blue eyes that twinkled like the lights on the bridge. He wore a brown sports coat with a white shirt and a thin black tie knotted tight to his collar. But the most distinguishing feature was his right hand. I saw emerging from his coat sleeve, a bulky bandage of thick white gauze covering his hand, exposing only the last two knuckles of each finger and the tip of his thumb.

"My name's Robert. What's yours?"

"Randy."

"Pleasure to meet you," he lifted his bandaged hand from the wheel and extended it in a handshake.

I carefully and nervously wrapped my fingers lightly around the gauze and then felt him vigorously shake my hand. "I can take you the other side of Little Rock, so I hope that'll help."

Little Rock? Oh yes! About a hundred and forty miles and halfway across the state! I was too tired to match the enthusiasm I felt with the response that escaped my lips. "Yes," was all I could manage. I realized the only time I'd slept was a couple of hours in the car with Sundance. I'd been awake for close to twenty-four hours, and walking across the bridge had consumed what little energy I had.

"Nasty day to be hitching. Fortunately for you, it's already clearing in Little Rock." It was the first weather report I heard since I left home, and it was encouraging.

"Good," I mumbled. I listened to the tires splashing on the wet pavement. Exhaustion quickly overtook me, and coupled with the hypnotic sound of the windshield wipers sweeping back and forth, back and forth, I slipped into unconsciousness.

◈

Opening my eyes was totally disorienting. *I'm in a car, but where and with who?* Country western music twanged from the radio as the driver tried unsuccessfully to stay on key as he sang along.

"Where am I?"

"Forty miles east of Little Rock." He turned down the radio.

My brain clawed back from desperately needed sleep as I sat up and saw the now undulating, wooded terrain pass by. The sun poked through broken clouds, casting moving patches of light across the greening landscape. "Robert?"

"That's right. You passed right out back there. You must've been exhausted."

"I still am."

"Rough night?"

"Let me tell you." I proceeded to describe my walk across the Mississippi.

"I don't know anybody who's done that. I'm impressed." He grinned. "But what made you do such a thing?"

Over the next thirty miles, I explained my purpose. He listened intently, nodded his head at different points in my story. "You can see why I passed out."

"Sure can. I'd say God's looking out for you." He gave me a broad, infectious smile.

I couldn't help but smile back. "Maybe God made you stop and pick me up."

"*God* has all sorts of tricks up His sleeve." The way he said God and the way he looked at me made me feel uncomfortable. I went to church as a kid, and I believed in God and agreed with his comment. But I'd experienced Jehovah's Witnesses trying to sell me on the *Watchtower* and Mormon missionaries delivering their doorway message. I expected some sort of Evangelical sermon to come next. *Maybe he wants to baptize me in a lake as the price of my ride.* I remained silent and waited to hear what he'd say.

"You've been looking at my hand," he held it up.

He was right. It was impossible not to notice. "What happened?"

"God's plan. I strayed, and he brought me back. This," he faced his bandaged palm toward my face, "is his sign. I work in an auto body and detail shop. Four months ago, I was using an industrial buffer to shine up a car. I don't know why it happened, but the buffer got away from me, got jammed up, and spun around with such force it took my hand right off."

"Holy shit!" I didn't expect to hear that. Though after working in the mines, industrial accidents weren't alien to me.

"They slapped a tourniquet on my arm and took me to the car. I told them to bring my hand with us, so they tossed it into a cooler with ice, and we went to the ER. When we got there, the doctor said there was nothing he could do with my hand. I told him, sew it back on. Doctor said it was a dumb idea because it would rot and fall off. I asked if there was any chance at all. He said there was a slim possibility, but if it did, I'd be lucky to get ten percent functionality, given all the nerves had been severed. I insisted he do it, and he finally agreed. I think just to shut me up. A couple days later, my wife came to pick me up at the hospital. When they discharged me, they said come back in a week.

"As my wife drove me home, she explained that after what the doctor told her the day of the accident, she started crying, but right away, she got on the phone. Called everyone at her church and told them to pray for me that my hand would heal and be useful again. She told them to call their friends too, who, in turn, called other friends at other churches in the area. My wife got several hundred people to pray for me twice a day for the week before going back to the hospital.

"When she drove me to see the doctor, she quietly prayed the whole time. After the doctor removed the bandages, he was surprised the hand wasn't green or something. But when he started testing my fingers, you should've seen the look on his face when he saw them moving." Robert grinned as he raised his hand and wiggled all his fingers and thumb. "I told him how many people were still praying for me. The doctor said he'd never have believed it. Heck, neither did I. He told me, based on his testing, he thought I could get back ninety percent functionality."

I listened and watched him manipulate his fingers. There was no reason to doubt Robert or think he was making up the story. I was stunned by his accident and recovery—yet I wasn't. I don't personally care for organized religion, but I believe in God's energy. The fact that Robert had so many people praying for him all at once, maybe somehow, they channeled that energy through powerful waves of prayer.

"God's plan. I'm happy to be back in church again. You know, Randy

. . .”

Here it comes.

“... as I listened to your story, I believe God must have a plan for you too. I can tell you believe, and He looks out for those who do. Despite your troubles, things could’ve been much worse. Last night He got you safely over the river.” That was it. Robert let it go at that. He didn’t mention another word about God, prayers, or church as we drove through the rolling hills swelling around us.

Spring foliage rippled in the breeze and glittered under the sun. Around noon we reached his exit on the west side of Little Rock, and he pulled over to let me out. Robert looked at me with his infectious smile and said, “Never forget, God is with you—always. Sometimes, you just need to listen more carefully.” He extended his right hand, and I took it with more confidence. “I wish you the best of luck.” Robert gazed skyward. “Look what a beautiful sunny day you have to be on the road.”

I regarded the blue vault overhead, dappled with cottony puffs. “Yes, it is.” I looked back through the window; our smiles met. “Thanks for the ride, Robert. Good luck with your hand, and thanks for the advice. I’ll try and listen better.” I stepped back and waved.

As he drove off, I thought about what had happened to him. He had affirmed my belief in the power of prayer, and I agreed that God must be looking out for me. But I tempered my thoughts and expectations. God was no genie of the lamp to grant my wishes. I’d learned that help comes at odd times in odd ways, and the experience of pain is often part of divine intervention. *But, what the hell, I sure hope that God will provide a ride that’ll take me across the country.*

One-hundred-sixty miles lay ahead to Fort Smith on the Arkansas Oklahoma border. Wispy cumulus clouds drifted overhead, and a pleasant breeze rustled the leaves alongside the highway. After the recent rain, it smelled like spring. I looked up. *It* is *a beautiful day*, I thought. My mind wandered, and gradually two thoughts merged. Robert’s comment that

God was looking out for me and what Judd had said about Moses struggling in the desert. Both of them pointed me toward the same conclusion that God often shows the way with a plan. *Robert? My guardian spirit? No way! He can't be what Judd talked about.* If I came across one who'd reveal my vision quest, I was sure it would be some sort of animal, like a rabbit or some other critter. I thought again of Robert and shook my head slowly. *I can't imagine that God, whatever his or her form, is the guardian spirit Judd meant.* The whole idea was somewhat unnerving, so I stopped thinking about guardian spirits and God. I looked down the highway and spoke to myself, "It's up to me, my brain, and my will to figure a way out of my financial mess. Divine inspiration's the thing of stories. I'm dealing with cold reality."

I waited nearly an hour before a car picked me up. The man took me about thirty miles, where I waited another half hour for another thirty-mile ride. The day progressed much the same. Wait thirty to sixty minutes, ride half an hour. Around 3:30 p.m., I got a ride in the back of a pickup truck headed just across the border into Oklahoma.

It was a pleasant ride lying under the late afternoon sun as the wind blew past. I thought again about Robert and the more immediate problems facing my journey to Tucson. Given how I got across the bridge, maybe God *was* looking out for me. So, I tried not to feel nervous despite the approaching end of the day. A third night standing in an empty world worried me, but I resolved to not dwell on it. *Yeah, right. Let's see how well I can do that at 2:00 a.m. out here.*

Arkansas's wooded terrain gave way to a noticeable thinning of trees as I approached Oklahoma. The sky was expansive and deep blue, the puffy cumulus clouds still drifting east as the sun moved toward the horizon that seemed to stretch on forever. I was approaching the Great Plains. A vast expanse, slowly rising until it reached the Rocky Mountains hundreds of miles away.

My ride let me off near Sallisaw, Oklahoma. The red sun merged with the distant horizon, and the clouds grew pink and then turned dull gray. Off to the east, the great terminator of the night sky approached. Despite the pleasant weather, the thought of another night on the roadside was depressing. I stood there, thinking about Kate and the kids. In a pre-cell phone era, it was not unusual to be out of communication for significant periods. My thoughts went to our small home, imagining Kate fixing dinner for the kids, getting Amy ready for bed, hoping Anne was cooperating, and her teething had passed. "I've got to figure something out," I said to the glowing western horizon. I tried to imagine what it might be, but all that came to me were scenes of working in the woods. I shook my head, attempting to dismiss the images. "If you're looking out for me, God, I hope you're not going to put me back in the woods."

Staring off into the fading afterglow, I wondered what Kate was thinking about me. Then as if on cue, "*Pain will come back to you ...*" entered my head as I thought about the approaching night. I pushed it from my mind and remembered what Robert said about God watching out for me and tried to listen more carefully.

Chapter 9

Eddie

HONK! HONK! I SPUN AROUND. A GREEN FORD STATION WAGON STOPPED BEHIND ME. I stood frozen a moment as I had with Sundance. Finally, I approached the car, leaned in the open passenger window, and saw a man who looked to be about thirty, wearing a denim jacket, tee-shirt, and jeans. He was a large muscular guy—larger than me—with thick wavy dark hair, a square jaw, and dark green eyes. He gave me a wide smile. "It's yo lucky day," he drawled.

"What?"

"I'm goin' to Phoenix and need sum company."

I stood there like an idiot. Unable to speak, I didn't move.

"Are ya deef?"

I stared blankly at him as his destination sunk in. *Phoenix. That's only one-hundred-twenty miles north of Tucson. That's over a thousand miles in one ride*. I yanked open the back door and tossed my pack inside, then sat next to the driver. "Thanks for the ride!"

"Ma name's Eddie Long. What's yurs?"

"Randy. I'm pleased to meet you."

"Where ya goin'?"

"Tucson."

"See?" He grinned. "I told ya it's yo lucky day."

Someone up there must like me.

Eddie pulled onto the highway and explained how he left the Memphis area about six hours earlier. He was grateful to have the company, especially with night falling. Having driven the upcoming stretch across Oklahoma, Texas, and New Mexico, I knew it was a difficult trip to drive alone in the dark.

"Grab yurself a beer from that cooler in the back and hand me one too."

I pulled two icy Budweisers, opened one and handed it to Eddie, and then popped the top and took a long swallow from my can. I relaxed into the seat and closed my eyes. It was spooky the way he suddenly appeared. *It can't be a coincidence. Can it?* Covering my bases, I thanked God for the fortuitous appearance of Eddie Long and avoiding another empty landscape for the third night. But I couldn't have imagined what my ride with Eddie had in store. "What takes you to Phoenix?"

"I gots a letter from ma gurlfriend, Julie-Sue, so I'm gonna fetch her back," he put the can to his mouth and looked at me. "She luves me. We're gonna git married."

How sweet, I thought. *Love's propelling him halfway across the country. This should be much better than riding with Sundance.*

Eddie started describing her in minute detail, short, curvy, long red hair, deep blue eyes, and a charming smile. They'd known each other for about ten years, and Eddie had missed her so much. I watched the guy talk with his thick Tennessee drawl and how he'd giggle like a little girl when he said something that struck him as funny. Eddie reminded me of Jethro from the *Beverly Hillbillies*. There was a genuine boyish charm in his manner, and I found myself readily liking him. He appeared to be a pleasant guy and someone whose company I could enjoy over the next twelve-hundred miles and eighteen hours.

Eddie finished his beer and tossed the can in the back seat. "That shore was good," he wiped his mouth with his sleeve. "I've missed beer almost as much as I've missed Julie-Sue."

Missed beer? What? "Where've you been that you missed beer?"

"Jail."

What the fuck? My brain was suddenly very confused. One moment I'm enjoying the charming guy's love quest, giggling about his girlfriend, then he says he's an ex-con. "Jail?"

"Yup."

"When did you get out?"

"Yesterday. They let me out on pa-roll 'cause I wuz real good when I wuz there."

"So, you're on parole?"

"Yup."

"Driving to Phoenix?"

"Yup."

"Does your parole officer know you're out of state?"

"Nope."

"But isn't that..."

"Yup. I'm via-late-in ma pa-roll." He looked at me and smiled.

Holy shit! God has a hilarious sense of humor.

"I don't care 'cause I'm in luv. Julie-Sue wrote me in jail. She tole me she's ma gurl an I'm her man." Eddie grinned and giggled.

Great. I'm driving in a car with a guy drinking beer who's skipped parole. If we should get stopped by the cops—

"I haven't seen her in two years since they put me away."

"That's a long time. When did she write and tell you to come and get her?"

"Almost two years ago. Julie-Sue didn't zactly say come git her."

"No?"

"I'm gonna sooprize her and jus' show up to her place in Phoenix."

Oh no. Is he out of his fucking mind? But I hadn't heard it all yet.

"Yup. Julie-Sue's gonna be so sooprized," he giggled again. "And so's Larry."

My curiosity piqued, I asked, "Who's Larry?"

Eddie didn't skip a beat. "Her husband."

"She's married?"

"Yeah, but she don't luv him."

"How do you know?"

"I jes know it. When I got outa jail yesterday, I went to her house. Her mama said she got married to Larry a year ago and moved to Phoenix. Her mama said she weren't so happy to go and wished she'd come home. So, I sez I'll fetch her back."

I tried to process the conversation, but it made my head hurt. Naturally, the big question on my mind was how he wound up in jail. Eddie seemed like a pleasant guy, so I didn't think asking would offend him. My guess was he got caught stealing a car. "So … Eddie. How come you were in jail?"

He giggled and slapped the wheel. "I had me a grudge to settle."

"With who?"

"Ya see, I live in Frayser. It's a small town north a Memphis, on the river. I gots all kinda family there. Brothers, sisters, uncles an ants, and lot's a cousins. Us Longs, we've lived there since befoe the Civil War."

I couldn't help but think about the classic hillbilly feud between the Hatfields and McCoys. "Some sort of family feud?"

"Well … you kin mee-be say that. This time the trouble started with ma brother Joe."

This time?

"Ma lil brother got his-self picked up for drunk and disorderly by Sid Johnston. He's named Sid 'cause his family's ree-lated to the famous Confederate General, Sidney Johnston. Anyway, ma dumb brother must'a said sumthin' that pissed off ol' Sid. Pissed him off real good, 'cause Sid started a whompin' on Joe, who was too drunk to fight back proper. Sid beat the crap outa Joe and put him in the hospital." Eddie's brow furrowed, and his head tilted to one side. "Now Joe done sumthin' dumb, and I'm shore Sid didn't like what Joe said. But that don't give Sid no right to bust up Joe like that. No sir. In a fair fight, Joe wood'a beat the snot outta ol' Sid. Hell, Sid only weighs 'bout two-hundret-n-forty."

Eddie paused, seemed lost in thought as he recalled the story. Wanting to know more, I grew impatient. "So?"

"Well, Sid made me mad. So, I had to do sumthin' bout what he done to Joe." As Eddie related the story, I watched him get more animated as residual anger crept into his otherwise pleasant voice. "This wuz a family fight 'cause them Johnston's got it again' us Longs for lot's a years. So … I went huntin' for ol' Sid one night. Knew he wuz on duty and where he'd be sittin' on his sorry ass. I saw his pole-eece car down by the river. I comes up from behind and sees his elbow stickin' out the win-da." Eddie giggled and nodded his head. "I walked right up to his win-da, reached out," he extended his powerful right arm, made a tight fist, and grimaced, "an I pulled that stupid sum bitch right thru the win-da afore he knew what wuz happenin'. I thru his sorry ass on the ground and gave him a whompin' he'll never forgit." I watched Eddie's powerful hands grip and twist on the steering wheel. "When I was satisfied, he wern't gettin' up, I picked him off the ground an hung him by his belt from one'a them climbin' spikes on'a telephone pole." He giggled again and looked at me. "Then ya know wut I done next?"

There's more? I just shook my head.

"I took that nice pole-eece car an drove it inta the river." He laughed hard.

"I guess the cops were pretty upset with you."

"Shit. I knew they wuz gonna a-rest me, so I saved 'em the trouble lookin' for me. I drove right ova to the pole-eece station an walked inta the desk sergeant an said, 'I jes beat the snot outa ol' Sid, left him hangin' on the phone pole, an ran his car inta the river. I s'poze y'all wanna a-rest me, so here I am.'" More giggles. "Yo shuld'a seen the looks on their dumb cop faces." He looked at me with a big grin and nodded his head. He was obviously proud of avenging his brother.

I was speechless. *This guy's crazy.* When I regained my wits, I asked,

"How much time did they give you for that?"

"Three years in the County farm. Shit. I didn' mind. I got to spend a lotta time with ma family. There wuz two uncles and six of ma cuzins doin' all sorts a time. Be-sads, I got to eat real good cuz one of ma uncle's the head cook. It wus what sum folks calls easy time."

I'd known colorful characters who'd stepped over the line with the law. Some even found themselves in jail, but nothing like this. It was so bizarre; I couldn't imagine this guy making it up.

Eddie wrinkled up his face. "Cept there wus one time I gots pissed off at a guy in ma bunkhouse."

Now what?

"It almost kept me from gettin' outa there on pa-role. It wuz Ralph York. He never liked me even when we wuz kids in school. It wuz 'bout a munth ago when he knew I wuz gitten' out on pa-role a year early. Ralph's family and ol' Sid's kin have been marrin' for years, so he didn' like what I done to Sid. He thought he'd pick a fight with me an fuck up ma pa-role. Well, I was shore ready to go. I'd stayed long enough an did all the visitin' I wanted. That Ralph jess kept' a needlin' me every day, tryin' to make me fight an get in trouble with the guards. Then one night he said somthin' 'bout my Mama I couldn't agnore. I hopped outa ma bunk bed, stood there an looked up at him, 'cause ol' Ralph, he's bigger 'n me. I tole him I had enough an he better not talk 'bout ma Mama no more. The big dumb shit stood there an laughed. Do ya know what ol' Ralph said to me?"

"I can only imagine."

"He called ma Mama a whore!" Eddie's face grew dark as he recalled the insult. "I jes took ma right fist," he held it up and shook it for emphasis, pulled his elbow back, and then swung straight up. "I punched him upside his chin as hard as I could, lifted him off the floor an he fell on his back out stone cold." He looked at me with a wicked grin before he finished his story. "I whomped him so hard I knocked a eyeball right outa his head. It just sorta hung down as he was passed out on the floor. I also busted up ma hand bones real bad."

When I heard the eyeball part, my first inclination was to think he was exaggerating to impress me. But then two things made me believe the guy. During the past winter, I took an advanced first aid class. Our instructor said when someone hits their chin with enough force on the steering wheel; an eyeball could pop out of its socket. If we encountered a dangling eyeball, put it in a paper cup, hold it to the victim's empty socket for transport. At the ER, they'll pop it back in. I also saw the knuckles on his right hand were deformed as if badly broken. I concluded he was telling the truth. Far be it from me to dispute his claim. Anyone who made Eddie Long mad did so at his own peril.

"So how come that didn't screw up your parole?"

"Ma uncle tole the guards Ralph slipped an fell real hard on his chin. Ya know, sum kinda ax-e-dent."

"But didn't Ralph tell them you punched him? One look at your hand and they'd know he was telling the truth."

"Well … Ma uncle, he picked Ralph off the flow when he come to. Ma uncle held that eyeball in his hand." Eddie giggled. "Poor Ralph went all to pieces seein' it there. Ma uncle made him promise to tell the ax-e-dent story, or he'd yank it right outta his head." He giggled and slapped the wheel.

Eddie's crazy story exhausted me. "Do you mind if I close my eyes for a while? I haven't had much sleep since I left New Hampshire."

"Y'all go right on an take a nap fur a while. But before you do, git me another beer."

Who was I to argue with this guy? I grabbed a Bud and handed it to him then closed my eyes. The image of Eddie's uncle threatening Ralph was the last thing I remembered before passing out.

◈

I napped as we drove through the night, waking just before we reached the Texas border. We passed through Amarillo around midnight, where he stopped to gas up the car. When we got back on the highway, Eddie asked, "So, why ya goin' to Tucson?"

It was time to talk to Eddie to keep him awake, avoid an accident, and stay alive. "Last week, it started with shoes."

"Shoes?"

I told him my worries about family and money that Kate was pregnant, and I was supposed to figure out a career plan. As I talked, Eddie listened attentively, periodically asking me questions. His first question was the usual one.

"How'd ya talk ur wife into lettin' ya come all the way out here an leave her alone with the kids?"

"She's tired of the money problems and knows my work history." I stared out the window at a tiny knot of lights in the infinite darkness, an infrequent sign of humanity in the flat Texas plains. "I guess I convinced her that I couldn't think in that madhouse and needed to get a long way away."

Eddie giggled and offered, "Maybe she wanted to get rid of you fur a while."

His suggestion slapped me. I felt uncomfortable considering that possibility for the first time. At that moment in our relationship, Kate and I had an *understanding*. For two years, we'd been dabbling with an open marriage and fooled around with a few other people. It sort of went with the era. Perhaps her change of heart to my plan was because she wouldn't be as lonely as I thought. Especially when her last instruction was, "Don't bring anything back with you."

The miles rolled by as we passed through Texas into New Mexico. We talked about all sorts of other things. It's what you do to keep awake, driving through the middle of nowhere on a practically empty highway in the dark, as the engine purred, tires droned on the pavement, and country music faintly played in the background. I talked about the challenges of raising so many kids and being a stepfather. I also told him about working in the woods and an underground copper mine.

"Yur crazy!" Eddie shook his head. "I can't imagine workin' in no hole in the ground. You gots sum balls to do that. And how kin ya handle so many kids runnin' round yur house?" My tales seemed to impress Eddie, and he appeared to respect me for what I'd done and was trying to do for my family. "I like you, Randy," he said with a toothy smile, showing his white teeth as he slapped the steering wheel again. I could tell this crazy hillbilly meant it. I suspected that if anyone beat me, Eddie Long would explain the error of his ways.

◈

Albuquerque, New Mexico, lay far behind as was the dawn that lit the eastern sky, silhouetting mountains against the growing light. We passed through desert lava fields, black, rough, and barren. Just across the Arizona border, we drove between low mesas that flanked I-40. Suddenly, a great dark gray shape emerged from behind a flat mesa on my side of the car. A giant B-52 bomber flew past, less than fifty feet above the highway, directly in front of us. Eight deafening jet engines roared and screamed, shaking the car. Suddenly it disappeared behind another mesa. The unexpected appearance of the giant, noisy bomber snapped us wide awake.

We reached Flagstaff just before 9:00 a.m. and turned south on I-17 for the remaining hundred and fifty miles to Phoenix.

"Ya know, Randy, I think you should stay with me ta'night at Julie-Sue's."

"I don't know about that." *Are you out of your mind? She doesn't even know you're coming. And you want to invite a guest?*

Eddie insisted. "It'll be fine with her."

"What about Larry?"

"Oh, he won't care none. Come on, spend the night, an tomorra I'll drive ya down to Tucson. Come on. Wadda ya say?"

It was a tempting thought. I could sleep under a roof and avoid hitching to Tucson. But the more persuasive argument was my morbid curiosity to see what would happen with the love triangle. "Okay. If it's alright with Julie, I'll stay."

Eddie smacked the wheel, "Hot damn! I wants Julie-Sue to meet ya and see how intrestin' ya are."

Chapter 10

Triangle

IT WAS AFTERNOON WHEN WE PULLED IN FRONT OF JULIE-SUE'S TWO-STORY, salmon-colored stucco apartment building. Eddie pulled out a piece of paper, checked the apartment number, and jumped out of the car like an excited kid. I waited politely. When Eddie saw I hadn't moved, he stopped. "Come on, Randy. Don't be shy. I'm shore she'll like ya real good."

I followed him to her door. Eddie knocked. He looked like an eight-year-old boy waiting to open a Christmas present. He practically vibrated with excitement. The door opened. A short, attractive woman with shoulder-length wavy blonde hair stood gaping at Eddie.

"Julie-Sue! I'm so glad to see ya!" Eddie leaned forward, wrapped his crushing arms around the stunned woman, and pulled her off the floor like a feather.

"What the hell are you doin' here?" Julie-Sue shrieked. "You're supposed to be in jail." There was no romance in her words. It was pure shock.

"I wuz good, so I got out a couple a days ago on pa-role an came right to see ya."

Julie-Sue struggled to get out of his embrace and stood on the floor, shaking her head. "No, Eddie! You're not supposed to be here." Then she glared at me. "And who the hell are you?"

"That's Randy. He's ma friend. I picked him up in Oklahoma, an we drove all night to git here."

"A hitchhiker?"

"Yep." Eddie clasped his powerful hand on my shoulder and rattled me. "He's ma buddy. I tole him he could stay with me here. Tomorrow I'm drivin' him down to Tucson." He didn't wait for an invitation and pushed me inside past a furious and very confused Julie-Sue.

"I can't believe you're here," she shouted, closing the door behind her.

"Where's Larry?" Eddie scanned the room.

"At work. He'll be home around five."

Eddie walked into the kitchen, opened the refrigerator, pulled out two beers, and handed me one. I stood there thinking, *I should just walk out of the door and hitch to Tucson.* But it was like watching a train wreck in slow motion. I couldn't look away. Eddie took a swig, walked back to Julie-Sue, grabbed her hand, and dragged her to the couch. He pulled her down next to him and wrapped his arm around her. "How's ma gurl? I missed ya so bad. But now I'm here an we kin be t'gether like ol' times."

I sat in the kitchen and watched Julie-Sue's face run through a range of expressions: shock, anger, confusion. "Why did you come here, Eddie?"

"'Cause I got yur letter. Ya said ya missed me, so here I am. Besides, yur mama said you was none too happy goin' to Phoenix. Now yur man's here to the rescue."

It struck me odd that Eddie didn't once ask her about marrying Larry. It seemed it didn't matter to Eddie at all. I kept watching her reaction, which slowly improved.

"You violated parole and drove all the way out here to get me?" She softened slightly.

"Shore thang, Julie-Sue. I luv ya," he leaned over and kissed her hair. Then he pulled back and furrowed his brow. "Wa'chya done to yur head, baby? How come ya cut yur beautiful hair an made it blonde?"

"Do you like it?" Now she smiled and primped her hair.

Eddie squinted, then smiled, "I could git use to anythang on you, Julie-

Sue." He ran his hand through her hair, and she giggled. Then Eddie giggled. Then he started to tickle her. Julie-Sue couldn't stop laughing as she tried to push away his strong hands.

I drank my beer, watching her transformation. Before I finished, Julie-Sue went from pissed to cuddling and making goo-goo eyes at Eddie.

The afternoon wore on. The couple talked on and on about what they both missed about each other. If it weren't for the fact her husband Larry would soon be home, the scene was quite touching. Hulking Eddie was like a little kid as he hugged and kissed her like a puppy.

Eddie got up for another beer with a big grin. "I tole ya so." He walked back to the couch and sat down. "So, I got's to git back before ma pa-role officer knows I'm gone, elstwize, I could go back to jail. How soon kin ya be ready to leave?"

Here it was. The big question I'd been waiting to hear asked and answered.

Without hesitation, she looked at him and smiled. "Tomorrow."

"Hot damn!" Eddie slapped his thigh. "So, to-marra mornin' after Larry goes to work, we'll drive Randy to Tucson an keep right on goin'."

"Goin' where?" Larry suddenly appeared in the room. He was a shorter but very stocky, muscular guy with thick tattooed arms bulging beneath a dirty t-shirt. Wiry brown hair pulled tight in a ponytail behind his head, with an angular face with icy blue eyes that glared at Eddie. "What the fuck are you doin' here, you stupid hillbilly?" spat Larry's deep angry voice.

Eddie jumped up. I braced for the explosive violence as he rushed at Larry with big hands opened wide; arms spread. Eddie grabbed Larry around the waist and lifted him off the ground. I cringed, knowing what the guy could do.

"Hey shit face," Eddie said, then suddenly the two men burst out laughing. The next moment they stood, vigorously shaking their strong hands, squeezing like vices, grinning at each other. "It's good to see ya,

Larry!"

"They actually let ya outta jail? How'd ya manage that?" Larry noticed me. "Who's he?"

"Ma buddy, Randy."

"Eddie picked him up hitchhiking in Oklahoma. He's going to Tucson." She walked to the kitchen and got a beer for Larry, smiling at her husband and then at Eddie.

Eddie and Larry began to talk like long lost friends. There wasn't the slightest tension between them, but I felt the electricity crackling between Eddie and Julie-Sue. I finished my third Coors when Larry ordered pizza and sent Julie out for more beer. Eddie told Larry about me, why I was hitching, and going to Tucson.

"Damn," Larry said to me. "You sound as crazy as Eddie, No wonder yur buddies."

Julie-Sue and the pizza arrived simultaneously, and we sat at the kitchen table, eating and drinking. Larry told me he was working at a construction job that he got through an Army buddy. I discovered Larry was a former Vietnam veteran. "What did you do?" I asked.

"Special Forces," Larry said with pride. "I used to git dropped in VC territory, an I'd kill as many Gooks as I could."

Eddie slobbered down a pepperoni slice, "Larry liked killin' an he wuz real good at it."

His friend blushed. "Oh, don't go tellin' Randy how I use to be. Now I'm all settled down here with ma be-u-tiful wife. Ain't she pretty?" he asked me.

"She's lovely," I said, feeling buzzed from the beer.

Larry squeezed her hand, "She knows I luv her more than anythang in the world. Don't cha Julie-Sue?" He looked at her; thick fingers cupped her delicate chin. "I'd kill anyone who messed with her." It was a statement of fact to be enforced by a trained and powerful killer. Julie laughed, then pinched Larry's cheek before she stood and went to the sink.

Eddie got up, took his plate to the kitchen, and handed it to Julie-Sue.

"D'ya know how to play hearts, Randy?" Larry asked me as he finished his fourth beer. His back was to the sink.

"Sure, do." I looked at Larry, but behind him I saw Eddie grabbing Julie-Sue's butt as she kissed his neck.

"Git the cards, Julie-Sue," Larry called out. "Let's play some hearts."

I've played cards under some weird circumstances, but never anything like that night, not before or since. We sat at the table. Larry was across from me, Julie on my right and Eddie on my left. We played for a couple of hours, drinking more beer and eating leftover pizza. Larry was getting pretty loaded, growing oblivious to his surroundings. I watched Eddie and Julie-Sue looking at each other, smiling and blowing air kisses. A couple of times, I felt them playing footsie underneath the table. I watched Larry with pity, a man about to be taken totally by surprise by his wife and a good friend. He was clueless and very drunk.

"Hey, Eddie," Larry slurred. "Screw work tomorrow. I'll drive down to Tucson with you guys to drop Randy off." I glanced at the two lovebirds for their reaction.

"You shouldn't miss work again." Julie-Sue cautioned. "You'll get fired,"

"Fuck the job. I wanna ride with y'all tomorrow."

"I don't wanna git ya inta trouble, Larry," Eddie said.

"No trouble, Eddie." Larry stood and swayed. "I gots to git to bed." He stumbled into his bedroom. I saw him flop onto the bed, face down.

I waited to see what Eddie and Julie-Sue would do now that they were alone.

"I hadn't planned on Larry coming with us," Julie quietly said as she wrapped her arm around Eddie.

"That's OK. After we drop Randy off, we'll come back here an git Larry drunk," Eddie chuckled. "Then, we'll take off when he passes out."

Julie-Sue giggled. "You're a bad boy, Eddie Long." She smiled. "I'm goin' to bed now. You two are welcome to the living room."

When she was gone, Eddie insisted I take the couch. He laid on the floor next to me, like some sort of faithful hunting hound dog. I wanted to ask him about the evening and his plans but declined. I didn't want to know. I feared what would happen when Larry found out Eddie and Julie-Sue ran off back to Tennessee. Would it be Larry's turn, like Sundance, to drive over a thousand miles on a murderous quest for vengeance? No matter how it went down, it would not be a pretty picture. I didn't want to be anywhere near it.

◈

The next morning, we climbed into Eddie's car and drove to Tucson. Pleasant conversation filled the two-hour drive, masking Larry's surprising future. Eddie pulled off I-10 at Speedway Boulevard, just north of downtown Tucson. He let me out at a Circle K where I could phone my former roommate Jack and let him know I'd arrived. Walking over to Eddie's window, I reached out to shake his hand—the eye-popper—and say goodbye and thank him for a long and entertaining ride across the country.

He grinned and said, "I'm shore glad I picked ya up." Then Eddie nodded his head sideways toward the back seat where the couple sat. He winked and flashed me a broad and knowing smile. As they pulled away, I longed to know how that love triangle would all turn out. It has remained a puzzling source of speculation throughout the rest of my life.

Chapter 11

Tucson

I RECONNECTED WITH MY FRIEND JACK THAT AFTERNOON. In the evening, we sat drinking Dos Equis amber beer at his rented house in the desert foothills. The Catalina Mountains dominate Tucson's northern landscape, and from his porch, we had a great view of them fading into the darkening sky. We hadn't seen each other since I left Arizona in 1974. Jack lit up a joint and was surprised when I reached out my hand for a hit.

"What's this?" He was shocked. "You don't smoke!" Jack handed it to me with a smile. After a few hits, I told him the story of when I finally got high for the first time.

All through high school, I'd resisted doing any drugs—except alcohol. I had always had ready access to all of it, but I had no interest. When in college, Jack and his friends kept trying to get me high, but with no luck. After I met Kate, she and her friends thought I was a stoner by how I looked and acted. When they discovered I was straight, they too made it their mission to get me high. Then one day, I picked up a hitchhiker who offered me some hash, and I tried it. The anonymous encounter allowed me to deprive any of my friends the distinction of claiming to be the first to get me high. I didn't smoke much, as I couldn't afford it, though it sure helped me cope with my kids' wild energy. By the time I finished telling the tale, I had a pleasant buzz from the beer and pot.

"How the hell did you get into your current fix?" The last time Jack had seen me, I was still single with no plans to get married and certainly no plans to become an instant parent. He shook his head. "I still can't believe you did that. Nobody you knew out here could." My reputation had been that of a wild and crazy guy. I lived on the edge. I drove around like a nut in my beat-up '63 MGB sportscar and worked as an underground miner. No one could picture me married, let alone with kids.

I shrugged my shoulders. "I didn't expect it. My sister introduced us, and it just sort of happened."

We reminisced about being dorm mates at the University of Arizona in '71 and then when we shared rental houses. He swigged from his beer and changed the subject. "So, what's your big plan?"

I looked at him blankly. "I haven't a clue."

"What?" Jack was dumbfounded. "You must have thought about it on your way out here. You had plenty of time with nothing to do."

"I was preoccupied. Spent most of the time focused on the journey. Yeah, I wondered what I'd come up with, but just kept rehashing my current situation. For some reason, I couldn't dig into the problem and work on a solution." I smiled at Jack, and glibly said, "I'll figure it out."

Jack laughed at me and shook his head. "You better or your wife'll kill you."

"I know." My smile vanished. "When I called her this afternoon, naturally, that was the first question. Not 'how are you,' but 'what's your plan?'"

"What did you say?"

"I'm working on it." I looked at the beer in my hand. "She sounded unhappy. It wasn't the answer she was expecting."

Jack laughed again. "Gee, I wonder why, you moron." His face grew severe. "Seriously, do you have any idea at all?"

"Nope." I leaned back in the chair, took another drink from my beer. "But I'm sure something will come to me." As if on cue, the one-hit radio station in my head began to broadcast that ever-popular refrain, *Pain will come back to you*. That was an understatement if I were to return with no plan.

◈

I finally got out of bed early the next afternoon, while Jack was at work. It was fantastic. I didn't have to think about getting a ride or being around some crazy love triangle about to spin out of control. I was free to get down to the business at hand.

After grabbing a bite to eat, I stepped outside into the familiar Sonoran Desert on a typical March day, with clear skies and very dry 80-degree weather. I looked at the saguaro cacti scattered around the foothills, their arms jutting in all sorts of positions, looking as if they were at a sporting event, waving excitedly for their team. From the desert floor sprung an assortment of other cactus, along with mesquite and paloverde trees. The familiar desert sounds of birds and insects surrounded and soothed me as I gazed at the Catalina Mountains, rising to ten-thousand feet, where snow still capped the highest reaches. I felt at home and comfortable in the desert, a place I loved and had spent much time hiking and driving around.

Alone, away from my noisy and crowded house, I was ready to think about my grand plan. And so I did.... But nothing happened.

It distressed me that my mind was a total blank—nothing. *I gotta come up with something*. Sitting on Jack's porch, I tried again to think, but my mind was a muddle. *I came all this way to figure out my career, but how do I begin? What can I do?* It made my head hurt, so I had to set it aside for the moment. *It'll come to me.*

I'd not felt such warmth since the end of the previous August, so I made myself comfortable and basked in the sun. It was glorious—

Oh, brother! *What kind of a bozo am I lounging around in the warm sun, doing nothing while Kate sits cooped up with the kids?* It would be months before she could relax and enjoy the warm sunshine. I chastised myself. *I must be some kind of selfish asshole!* The oppressive weight of guilt diminished the pleasure of the sun, deflating my good mood. Slumping in the chair, I thought, *I have no right to enjoy myself.* I was supposed to be in a crucible, succumbing to the firey pressures of adversity, busy purging my mind to fulfill my vision quest—

Hold on one damn second! What the hell have I been doing the past two years? Working my ass off to support my family!

I sat upright. "I have no reason to feel guilty!" I earned that moment in the sun, considering what I'd done to support my family. Sure, I had a full-time graphics job for a while, did a bit of freelance illustration, and some road construction. However, I'd spent the bulk of my employment energy working in the woods cutting cordwood at that farm in Dublin. One summer, I worked with my partner Ralph, and we produced a pile four feet tall, four feet wide, and 100 yards long.

I mentally calculated what that meant. A cord of wood is four by four by eight feet, cut split, and stacked—each cord of green hardwood weighs over 5,000 pounds. I had picked up each piece at least three times between cutting it and stacking it on the trailer, then unloading and stacking it along the road. That meant I lifted over 15,000 pounds for each cord—seven and a half tons total! I was responsible for half that pile, which meant I'd picked up over a quarter-million pounds of wood.

After that summer's work, I felt totally justified. But when I thought about working alone during the winter, I felt damn defiant if anyone—including myself—suggested I should feel guilty enjoying the warmth.

Cutting cordwood was difficult enough during the summer. Working through the winter was brutal. I had to drive forty minutes each way in our old Chevy van with a lousy heater, then work six to ten hours a day in temperatures that could drop to 10-degrees below zero, often wearing snowshoes. My lunch usually froze, which I had to try and thaw out, and my mustache and beard iced up. Because the van's heater was so bad, I'd arrive home with icicles still hanging on my face. That winter, I produced an additional fifteen cords, representing an additional 110 tons of wood moved. I forced myself to do this work, day in and day out, to support my family. When that was the only work I could find, that's what I did. Then, when I was home, I still had to be outside dealing with firewood for the house, which meant cutting, splitting, stacking, and carrying wood into the house to burn in the stove.

"No! I earned my place in the sun, and I'm damn well going to enjoy it."

Later that day, I thought about the career problem again. I wracked my brain to try and create a workable plan but found myself getting nowhere. *I'll just come back to this problem later.* After all, I was in Tucson, the "Land of Mañana." *Why do something today I can put off 'til tomorrow?* I fell into the attitude that poorly served me in high school and college—procrastination. But before I put the problem aside, I did manage to reflect deeply on my life and take stock of what I had to work with. The known quantities of my life would guide me to develop a workable plan.

I wasn't an academic and never learned how to be a student, so I wound up limiting my career options. I never rebuilt the bridges burnt in school. After dropping out of college, I tried to make my way in the world as a maintenance man and commercial artist. My jobs often switched between commercial art and physical labor, and I'd never held a full-time job longer than six months. These were my professional skills, experience, and baggage that I had to consider. It was a very limited toolbox. *What sort of stable and rewarding career can I pull from that mess?* It was distressing. Faced with such a daunting challenge, I immediately descended into familiar procrastination.

◈

Almost three weeks slipped by, during which time I applied myself to the I-hope-something-will-come-to-my-mind philosophy. I spent lots of time hiking in the desert, staring into the abyss of my mind, empty of any workable clue of what to do. I visited old friends, who'd ask the same questions as Jack, "What's your plan?" To which I couldn't answer because there was no answer to my dilemma. I went to some parties and bars, got treated to drinks and joints as I told my story. I amazed and entertained former and still single friends with my incomprehensible tale of married life with four kids. All of which afforded me a kind of celebrity—or curiosity—that helped me relax and forget my troubles back in Marlow. However, it did nothing to solve my career problem. It wasn't for lack of trying but think as I did, nothing came to me. I grew depressed as the ugly face of failure stared at me.

Each time I called Kate, I had to keep it very vague. After I asked her how things were going, the conversation usually went like this:

"What's happening?" she'd ask.

"I'm working on it."

"On what?"

"The plan."

"What is it?"

"I can't quite explain it yet."

"When are you coming back?"

"Soon."

Soon got closer and closer, yet I was no closer to solving the problem. My time in Tucson was nearly up, and I had to head home. After hitching west, I wasn't looking forward to hitchhiking back to New Hampshire. Hoping to avoid that prospect, I went to the Student Union building on the University of Arizona campus and checked the message board where people posted "rides" and other messages. The solution to the hitchhiking problem stared me in the face. RIDER FOR DRIVE AWAY WANTED.

I looked at the destination. Youngstown, Ohio. *That's on the Pennsylvania border. Oh yeah! That'll get me within six-hundred miles of home.* A drive-away was when someone wanted to fly home and have somebody else drive their car back. It sounded perfect, so I wrote down the name and phone number and that night called Barney.

"Hello? Is this Barney?"

"Yeah."

"Still need someone to ride with you back to Youngstown?"

"Yeah."

Talkative, I thought. *This could make a long drive seem even longer.* "When are you leaving, and what are you driving?"

"A girl I know wants me to drive her little Fiat sedan. I'm leaving the day after tomorrow. Interested?"

"You bet!" I explained my situation and how I preferred only to hitch a few hundred miles to get home.

"Okay. She's covering gas money. You drive when I'm tired. I'm planning on driving straight through." That was it. Barney explained where to meet him in two days.

I called Kate and told her, "Great news."

"You figured out your plan?" She was relentless.

"I think so," I lied and immediately changed the subject. "I found a ride almost back to Pennsylvania. I won't have to hitch most of the way."

"Okay." Like a naval destroyer hunting an enemy submarine, she tacked back onto her implacable course. "But what's your plan?"

"I'll tell you when I get home in a few days. I promise." She replied with an extended period of silence. "You still there?"

"You better have something."

"Oh, I will. Don't worry." I hung up slowly. *I better figure out something before I get back. I have to.* I knew that her time alone with the kids had to have been incredibly stressful. I needed to get my ass home fast and help with all the chores that she'd handled by herself.

It was one thing not to feel guilty about basking in the sun when I first arrived. But it had been almost three weeks! I'd be a liar if I said I wasn't having one hell of a great time. I was away from home, hanging out with old friends, partying, drinking, and smoking. *What if I don't go back?* After all, I'd fallen back into my pre-marriage lifestyle—except for sex—

and loved it.

If I wanted to be a selfish asshole, the opportunity was at hand. In fact, some friends questioned my sanity for going back to what I'd escaped. Maybe if I actually had a plan, I'd feel better about returning to the chaos. However, since there was no plan in sight, I realized my prolonged absence could easily—and rightly—be construed as just a bullshit joyride and grounds for divorce at a minimum, and even justifiable homicide were distinct possibilities. At that moment, the thought of abandoning my family was mighty attractive. It was an idea that I probably gave about ... thirty seconds of delightful consideration.

I had come to Tucson because I felt it was necessary for my family's survival, which was no longer just three stepchildren, but a daughter of my own and another child on the way. It was now my family as much as it ever was Kate's, and I believed marriage and family are the most serious commitments one can make. I'd desperately wanted a family, which got me into marrying Kate—right or wrong. However, once committed, I'd do absolutely anything to support them, even if it meant hitchhiking 6,500 miles at no small risk to reinvent myself and launch a new lucrative career. I did it because I felt it was the right thing to do, and there was no turning back or running away. I had to "face the music," regardless of whether I ever came up with a plan or not.

My last night at Jack's house was uneventful. "So, what's your plan?" he queried.

"Not you too," I complained. "That's all I hear from Kate."

"What do you expect? You've been on vacation in sunny Tucson, and she's been stuck back there in cold New Hampshire with four kids."

"I know, you're right." I felt like shit about it, but that didn't change the fact I still had no plan.

"Are you nuts? Don't tell me you don't have anything yet?"

"Afraid so."

"You're a dead man." Jack shook his head, then looked at me. "Maybe you better stay here until you figure it out."

"No. I need to go back. I can't leave Kate alone any longer."

"Your funeral."

"Pain will come back to you." Yeah. She'll break every bone in my body.

"Well, I have a present for the condemned man." Jack handed me a brown paper lunch bag.

"What is it?" I asked, peering inside.

"I baked you some special brownies for the road. Should make the drive more interesting."

I smelled the herbal contents and smiled. "What a thoughtful present, Jack."

"I think it's because I feel sorry for you."

Chapter 12

Barney

AT 8:00 A.M., JACK DROVE ME TO MEET BARNEY. As we arrived, my traveling companion stowed a duffle bag into the small cream-colored Fiat sedan. He was nothing like I expected. Here was another old-school hippy that looked like he could have been Sundance's brother. Barney was about my height but chunkier, with long curly red hair down to the middle of his back and a matching six-inch beard. I figured Barney to be close to thirty. He wore a ratty tee-shirt, cutoff shorts, and sandals.

"Looks like the brownies were a good choice," Jack said, eying my ride as I got out of the car.

I nodded slowly and turned back to my friend. "Thanks for putting me up." We shook hands through the window of his car.

"Good luck," he said. "If I don't hear from you, I'll assume you didn't come up with a plan, and you're dead." He chuckled and drove off.

"Hi, Randy," Barney said as I approached the car. "I'm ready to leave."

"Excellent." I put my pack in the car and sat in the passenger seat.

"Looks like good weather ahead," he reported and pulled out of the driveway.

We headed to I-10, which would take us east toward New Mexico and Texas. As we drove, I pleasantly discovered Barney was more talkative than I thought. We began with the usual introductions, where we came from, and where we were going.

“You know, man,” Barney said after I told him why I was on the road, “you’ve been gone almost four weeks and still have no plan.” He snickered. “Your old lady’s gonna kill you when you get home.”

“She will if I don’t have a plan.” I was sick and tired of the standard observation. I didn’t need anyone to tell me what I knew only too well.

“But you don’t have anything.”

“I know, I know.” I shrugged my shoulders. “What can I say?”

“You better hurry, and it better be good. ‘Cause you’re dead meat.”

“Thanks for your concern. I’ll think of something.” I reached into the paper lunch bag that crinkled as my fingers searched. “Well, to help me think, how ‘bout some brownies?”

◈

The Arizona and New Mexico desert along I-10 was familiar ground. I’d driven across that terrain nine times. Periodically, jagged mountains jutted from the desert floor, typical of the Basin and Range geology of that part of the world. After living back east for four years, I’d missed the huge vistas and gigantic sky and knew I’d miss it again as I got farther east and into the plains. Despite the beauty, it was still a tedious drive, so conversation helped make the miles pass.

“I’ve been in Oregon,” Barney explained. “Up in the Cascades hangin’ with a bunch of other freaks on a farm,”

Sounds like Hidden Springs, I thought. “How long were you there?”

“Three years. I got sick of the place. Nobody wanted to do shit. Just hang out and get high.” Barney shook his head, causing the mane of red locks to flutter over his shoulders. “Now, don’t get me wrong, I don’t have anything against gettin’ high. But I like to accomplish things. I froze my ass off last winter, and that was enough. That’s why I went to Tucson to warm up and collect my stuff.”

“Stuff?”

“Yeah. On my way to Oregon, I stayed with friends in different places and ended up leaving shit behind. So, now I wanna collect it."

"Speaking of shit. I hear they grow some killer weed up there."

"Yeah, but I've had better. I still got some stashed around I wanna pick up on the way back."

Barney spent the next eighty miles talking about all the fabulous pot and drugs he'd done over the years. I took it as typical BS, the same way fishermen brag about imagined catches or the ones that got away, growing larger with each telling. I didn't care. It was fun hearing how excited he got about his *stuff*.

"I got some great Tai sticks I wish I had for this drive," he lamented, and then went on to describe the quality and duration of the high the way a fine-wine connoisseur describes an exceptional vintage.

I told him about Hidden Springs, and we found ourselves comparing the typical flakes who hang out at such places, making their rounds to various communes across the country. Our similar experiences sounded only too familiar. As it was with Eddie Long, our bonding began, making the long trip that much more pleasant.

I hadn't bothered to ask Barney about his proposed route to Youngstown. I imagined we'd either continue on I-10 and across Texas's width or head up to Albuquerque and across I-40. After about four hours of driving, as we approached Las Cruces, New Mexico, Barney revealed his route.

"On my way to Oregon, I went through Texas and left some of my stuff there."

"Where?" I queried.

"Brownsville," he said casually.

Being pleasantly stoned, I nodded. The destination didn't sink home. I closed my eyes and visualized the shape of Texas. A huge state. Directly ahead of us, on the far western tip of the state, was El Paso. Driving across the middle of Texas would take us through Dallas and out the other side at Texarkana, the easternmost border 820 miles and 12 hours away. Another route across Texas was to head north to Albuquerque, New Mexico, and cross through Amarillo, covering about 120 miles of Texas. Then I visualized the southern extreme, that little point, way down at the bottom, the southernmost place in the continental U.S., *Brownsville, down on the Mexican border on the Gulf of Mexico—*

"Brownsville!" I sat up and looked at Barney. "We're going to Brownsville?"

"Sure."

Holy shit! I looked out the window. *"Pain will come back to you,"* surfaced once again in my mind. I realized the long ride had just increased by more than 600 miles. Going to Brownsville would take us across the bottom of the state through Laredo and along the Rio Grande, following state roads through some very desolate stretches for some eight-hundred miles and at least twelve hours of driving. Then back up through Houston to Texarkana for another 600 miles and ten hours. What could I do? I was literally along for the ride, so I grabbed another brownie as we drove through El Paso, then headed down toward Laredo.

◈

We covered much of our trip to Brownsville during the night, and traffic was sparse to nonexistent on the two-lane state road. After I napped for a while, just south of Del Rio, Barney had me drive so he could get some sleep. I felt insignificant following the cones of light, illuminating dashed yellow lines that slid hypnotically past the Fiat. *The stars at night, indeed, shine big and bright deep in the heart of Texas.* The night concealed the empty terrain from view. Periodic lights from lonely ranches or clusters around small towns were the few visible signs of an isolated population.

Barney snored next to me in a rhythmic counterpoint to the endless stream of dashed yellow lines. My mind wandered to home, Kate and the kids. The emptiness amplified the longing for my family, and I wished the trip was over. *Soon enough. Two or three days—*

Yikes! What will I tell Kate? The career board in my mind remained stubbornly blank after nearly a month. I leaned forward over the wheel and gazed up at the Milky Way and an array of other glittering stars. *Where the hell is my guardian spirit? I certainly won't find it driving through the underbelly of Texas.*

I pushed back in my seat, shifting my tired body, stiffening my arms against the wheel to stretch and ward off fatigue. *I can't go back to the woods.* I leaned forward again, looking up; *God, please don't send me back to the woods,* I pleaded with the same sincerity and desperation as I had for a ride outside of Hazleton. My mind was as blank as the void surrounding that deserted road. Alone with my thoughts, my fingers gripped the wheel as fear of failure slithered into my mind. *Everyone's right. Kate'll kill me. Worse still, she'll divorce me. This trip's been a colossal waste of time. I had no right to do it and leave her home alone to take care of the family. I'm a terrible husband and father.* Out of the gloom, I thought of Robert's advice. "Sometimes, you just need to listen more carefully."

I tried to empty my mind of fear and listen. *Okay. I hear Barney snoring, but I don't think that's telling me anything.* The Fiat's little four-cylinder engine purred along, turning at a steady 2,000 RPMs as displayed by the tachometer's needle. *Nope.* As I tuned out Barney and the engine, only silence remained. *I guess I'm not supposed to listen with my ears.* I looked inward, searching for a sign. Any sign at all. Still nothing. *Deeper. Go deeper.* I strained, grasping for anything—

It was faint. Something was definitely there. I detected an imperceptible voice from the void of my mind, just as the Fiat was an insignificant speck in the surrounding night. *Listen carefully.* It grew slightly, faint, but I felt there was something there. I concentrated, and the volume increased, became audible. *There it is! Yes. Distinct. What's it telling me?* Suddenly, with sparkling clarity, the inspiration I'd sought for thousands of miles, a voice spoke to me with a sense of authority. "You're a thoughtless moron. She's gonna kill you." *Thanks, God. Nothing like divine confirmation of what I already know.* The night and the road stretched endlessly before me.

◈

Early the next morning, we arrived in Brownsville and made our way to his former house near the coast. The smell of salt was in the air, which was a pleasant change from the dry desert I'd been in for several weeks. A red VW Bug sat in the driveway.

"Wait here, I'll be back," Barney said, heading for the front door. I watched him knock. When there was no answer, he banged louder. A few moments later, it opened, and a sleepy woman appeared, trying to identify the visitor.

"Barney!" she screamed. "You got a lot of nerve. Get out!" She tried to slam the door, but Barney put his foot in the way.

"Come on Lorie, lemme in."

"You worthless piece of shit!" She pushed with all her might and squashed his foot.

"Ow! That hurts."

"Serves you right."

"I'm sorry."

"Fuck you! Get out!"

"I don't blame you for being mad at me. All I want to do is get my stuff and leave."

"Like you did before?" Her voice grew icy.

"Let me explain. Please let me in." Barney's voice grew quiet, and I couldn't make out what he said. She finally opened the door and let him inside.

After half an hour, he emerged carrying a green duffel bag and a brown suitcase. *I hope they're not filled with drugs.* All I needed was the cops pulling us over and getting busted. Barney opened the trunk and tossed his stuff inside, and then climbed back in the car. He smiled at me. "All set."

Naturally, I was curious. "Can I ask what that was all about?"

We pulled away, and Barney replied, "I came down here and lived with Lorie for a year. Then one day, one of my friends called and invited me to Oregon, so I left."

"So, she was mad when you said you were leaving?"

"Actually, when Lorie was at work, I just walked out. I left a note on the table."

"No wonder she was mad!" I couldn't help thinking how friends had advised me not to go home—essentially walking out on my own family. I empathized with Lorie, even though all she had left to deal with was Barney's junk.

"I sent her a letter explaining why I left, and if she'd please hold onto my stuff. I wasn't sure if she had or if she burned it instead."

"She had no idea you were coming?"

"Right."

"You didn't know if she saved your stuff?"

"Uh-huh."

"So, we may have made this detour for nothing."

"Yeah," he smiled. "But, she saved it."

"What was so important you risked coming this far out of the way?"

"You know how it is. You get attached to things." All he did was smile. He never revealed what was so important or valuable, and I didn't press it any further. If he wanted to tell me, he would.

We drove north, heading for Houston. There was no Interstate highway for this leg of our journey. From Brownsville to Texarkana was about 650 miles traveling the two-lane state and U.S. roads. Houston was about halfway, and as we passed through the city, the car made an odd sound that slowly grew louder. "Do you think we should check it out?" I asked.

"Maybe next time we stop for gas. It's not my car anyway." Barney shrugged his shoulders.

However, within ten minutes, the noise grew so loud he had to stop. We both looked under the car. “Look at that,” Barney said casually.

I saw it too. There was a gaping hole in the small muffler. “So, what are you going to do?”

“I’m hungry,” Barney said, getting in the car. When he started the engine, it was deafening. “I can’t do anything about it,” he shouted, “so let’s eat.”

We had twelve-hundred miles to go with a blown-out muffler. It was painfully loud. Our conversation required shouting as the four-cylinder engine exhaust blasted through an ever-enlarging hole directly beneath my seat. As a result, conversation became less frequent, and we consumed the rest of my brownies.

Chapter 13

Farmers

THE DRIVE WAS UNEVENTFUL, EXCEPT FOR THE TERRIBLE ENGINE NOISE. But it sure beat hitchhiking. We made excellent time, and I periodically drove when Barney needed a nap. As we neared Memphis, I told Barney about my walk across the Mississippi and the man with the bandaged hand. When we approached the west end of the bridge, I looked at my watch. It took just over two minutes to reach the other side.

Suddenly, out of nowhere, Barney said, "I got to pick up more stuff."

I looked at him, disappointed we'd have to spend even more time in the noisy car. "Where?"

"Beyond Louisville, Kentucky."

He didn't say what he had to pick up, and the muffler was so loud that I didn't want to ask. So, I just accepted it.

"It won't be much of a detour," he shouted. After the run to Brownsville, there wasn't anything that could come close to that.

We continued onto Nashville, where we turned north on I-65 toward Louisville. The highway passed through low rolling hills with fields and trees. At Louisville, we got on I-71 that headed to Cincinnati, Ohio. It was a beautiful afternoon with a clear blue sky covering a land well into spring. It was now April, and all signs of winter had vanished from the landscape. We dropped down into the Kentucky River valley and followed the river south into farmlands until we headed up another smaller valley.

Eventually, we turned off on a dirt road that took us up a long hill. When we reached the top, the terrain was flat—like a mesa—but around the edges, there were many places where small valleys eroded down to the river below.

There were farms scattered around as the roads we took seemed to get smaller and narrower until we bounced down a gravel road following a wooded ridge of hardwood trees. We passed what looked like tobacco fields. The way got progressively worse, and I thought we'd end up on a cattle path, but a farm appeared over a rise. There was an old gray weathered two-story farmhouse, with plywood covering a few broken windows. It looked like it probably dated back to the early 1800s. There was a large gray barn bigger than the house, surrounded by several other outbuildings. Barney hadn't told me what to expect.

Barney continued, and the cattle path became the driveway where several broken hulks of cars and trucks lined the dirt path. There was a pen with goats. Chickens ran wild between the barn and the house. A functioning looking old dump truck and a rusted VW Microbus sat in the yard along with an old Ford tractor. Several small barefooted children and barking dogs ran toward the loud car, followed by a few adults.

He stopped the Fiat and mercifully shut off the engine, my ears still ringing. After his reception in Texas, I felt uneasy arriving unannounced in the middle of nowhere as four adults cautiously approached the car. Two men, who looked to be thirty-something, were dressed in denim bib overalls with dirty tee-shirts, work boots, with grimy John Deere ball caps cocked back on their head, with short black hair and matching beards. The two barefoot women wore peasant blouses and wraparound paisley skirts, each with a long braid down her back.

"Are we at the right place?" I asked nervously, my ears still ringing from the nonexistent muffler.

"Yep." Barney climbed out and spread his arms wide.

When they recognized him, it was all smiles and open arms of warm greetings.

"Barney! Ah can't believe it's you," said one of the men as he dispensed a bear hug. The four adults surrounded Barney with hugs, handshakes, and the women planting warm kisses on his cheeks. I got out of the car and walked toward the group. Barney introduced me, and I also received warm hugs from the women, and the med dispensed hearty handshakes and broad smiles.

"Y'all cum in-sad an git sumthin' to eat," offered one of the women.

We stepped inside to a level of clutter that made me feel right at home, and I longed for the confusion and chaos of my own home in Marlow. More kids greeted us, and, in the kitchen, I saw two more women who looked much like the others. It felt just like Hidden Springs, though I wasn't surprised given how Barney looked and what he described of Oregon. We were fed homemade bread, vegetables from the previous season, pork chops from their pigs, and apple pie, and all washed down with hard cider and local moonshine. Everyone sat around the big table as Barney told them what he'd been doing since he left them and went to Brownsville nearly five years ago. I felt relaxed from the food and drink, relieved to be sitting stationary in relative silence.

One of the women sent her kids out to play and then sat down, offering me more pie. She asked why I was with Barney, so I recounted the familiar story of leaving Kate with the kids. As she looked at me with wide eyes, I realized this was the first mother who'd heard my story.

"How can you do that? She's crazy too. Lettin' you go off like this, leavin' her stuck with the kids. An pregnant too!"

"I really can't argue that," was all I could manage, tired as I was.

She looked at me with narrowed eyes, perhaps taking my response as flippant. Maybe, as a mother, she took it personally and identified with being left alone to take care of the kids. However, I was in no mood to explain myself to a fleeting stranger. I was seriously road burned and buzzed from the moonshine, so I just let her think as she wished.

She then asked the usual question, "So, what's yur plan?"

I swallowed hard. "I don't know."

"Y'all don't know? Why, sweetie, yur wife's gonna kill you." She scowled. "I know I would."

Now I was pissed. *If I hear another person tell me Kate's gonna kill me, I'll—*

"So, where's my stuff?" Barney asked the woman, rescuing me from the inquisition.

She stood. "Shore thang. Right where you left it afor you went to Texas."

"I'd really like to stick around and visit," Barney said as he got up from the table. "But I gotta get this car to Youngstown, and Randy's gotta get back to New Hampshire."

Barney and I followed two men outside to the tobacco barn used for drying their crops. We entered the barn and climbed the stairs to the upper level. Instantly, My nose detected a familiar odor. *That's not tobacco*. At the top of the stairs, two more bib-overalled men greeted us and hugged Barney. They wore face masks, and I saw why. Behind tobacco plants, hanging from the rafters, there were hundreds of pot plants. Hidden Springs sold cordwood and lumber for cash. This group of hippies sold tobacco and pot.

I followed Barney into a small room to an old dusty three-drawer bureau. He opened the bottom drawer, which squeaked unpleasantly, and removed an old shirt, then pulled out a little bundle of red flannel. I watched with curiosity as he laid it on a dirty table and unwrapped it with reverence to reveal a small tan metal tackle box. He opened it and smiled, then turned it around so I could see the contents—his legendary stash of Tai sticks. Just as he'd described as we drove across New Mexico, which now seemed so far away, his drug stash story was as accurate as Eddie telling me he punched the eyeball from the annoying guy's head in the county jail. Barney opened the plastic bag, sniffed the aroma, then held it out to me.

"I think this was worth the detour." Barney grinned.

Anxious to get on our way, we headed back to the car. We made our goodbyes all around. One of the women handed Barney a basket with bread and a pie, followed by a lengthy kiss. Before we got in the Fiat, Barney shared a pipe full of his prized stash with me and the knot of adults surrounding the car. When I got inside, and Barney started the engine, the blown muffler's effects were softened by Tai stick attitude adjustment. The little sedan roared out of the driveway amidst waving adults, jumping children, barking dogs, and running chickens. We rewound our way through the now progressively widening and improving roads until we were once again on I-71 heading for Youngstown, some three-hundred miles away.

Chapter 14

Columbus

DRIVING THROUGH THE NIGHT, scores of red taillights ahead of us mixed with oncoming white headlights. Unlike the drive through desolate south Texas, this highway was alive with traffic as we approached urban Columbus, Ohio. Barney focused on the road, and I leaned back against the seat. Between the buzz from Barney's Tai weed, the car's roar, and general road burn from the long drive, my mind floated in an altered state of consciousness. I reflected on the journey and how I'd be back in Marlow within two days. When I saw the kids running around the hippy farm, I was anxious to get home and put the trip behind me. After nearly a month, I felt homesick for my family and looked forward to the kids' dull roar as a pleasant alternative to the muffler.

I wanted to relieve Kate from her solitary burden and smiled at the thought—

"*Pain will come back to you*," suddenly crashed into my mind, sending me into a terrible panic.

I sat bolt upright. "Two days? I'll be back in two days!"

"What's that?" Barney shouted above the muffler.

"I'll be back home in two days."

"Yeah. That's great. Back with your wife and kids."

And Kate will ask—no, demand—what's my grand plan. My heart pounded. I'd had nearly four weeks to figure it out, yet during that entire time, I may have focused a cumulative three hours on the problem. Yes,

I'd mulled the question over. Generally, I'd thought about it, but the total effort hadn't resulted in anything remotely workable. While driving through Texas the previous night, my failed attempt to listen more closely didn't help. It just scared me. The meaning of the song—now continuously playing in my head—became obvious. *Pain alright. There'll be a world of pain if I show up empty-handed. Like everyone says, she'll kill me.* My procrastination had run its course. Suddenly, I was in desperate deadline mode—with the operative word being dead. With wet palms and a dry mouth, panic consumed me as the refrain repeated like a nightmarish broken record.

Focus. Focus, damn it! Get control. Think! I had to think fast. Had to come up with something to justify leaving New Hampshire. I was desperate.

Then I remembered my wife's Lamaze child-birthing class. I took deep, cleansing breaths. *Breathe, damn it, breathe.* I suspect Barney was too focused or stoned to notice my labored breathing. *Breathe.* Slowly the veil of fear lifted, and the first relevant thoughts crept in. *How do I begin?... Where do I start?... I'm broke!... I don't have any real prospects, skills, or experience to support my family adequately.* My lack of education and work history stared me in the face. Panic returned, but I fought back. *Think! I need a steady job that pays enough to thrive—not merely survive.* That was a big duh moment if ever there was one. *Restating the problem's no solution, idiot! Dig deeper. I need to channel my altered consciousness from the muffler's white noise and the Tai stick. Maybe I can transcend reality and get a new perspective.*

I closed my eyes and fought to extinguish the taunting and distracting musical refrain. I recalled Robert's observations and advice. "Never forget God is with you—always. Sometimes you just need to listen more carefully." *Okay, okay. I'll try again and listen.* The blatting engine, like a tortuous white noise, drowned out everything. *I can't stop it, so work with it. Listen to the noise. Maybe God's trying to tell you something.* I accepted the noise and did my best to relax in the seat.

Ever so slowly, the loud exhaust began to sound more like a huge waterfall. I managed to relax into it, and an odd sense of calm enveloped me. In a flash, as if throwing a switch, my mind was clear, sharp, and focused. Within that calm, I detected a faint voice that said, *If you were independently wealthy and didn't need to work, what would you do with your time?* Even though I lived the polar opposite of financial independence, the question was worthy of investigation.

At least this voice seems to be more helpful than last night. I delved deeper into the underlying purpose of the question. *What would make me happy?* This was a critical question, considering I'd never held a job longer than six months. I needed something that I liked so that I would stick with it and become successful. Suddenly, the answer struck like lightning. *I'd animate cartoons to music!* The unexpected thought reverberated in my mind, like a thunderclap rolling through the mountains.

Okay. The answer surprised me, *but that's a start. Work with it.*

My love for Disney's original *Fantasia* ran deep. That was something I'd always wanted to do. Animate to music. However, my answer was equally abstract. *I need something tangible and substantial.* My mind began to process the situation. *I'm not independently wealthy, so obviously, I have to work. But I need a career—not merely a job—with the potential to earn enough money to support a family of seven.* I was onto the glimmer of something at last, so I pressed forward. *How do I turn this into a practical solution?* I adjusted my body in the seat.

Okay, animating to music could be a career. But how the hell do I get there?

I have no animation experience. That's an inconvenient fact. Sure, I understood animation was a sequence of twenty-four drawings for every second of film. Yeah, I'd watched countless cartoons, but actually producing an animation? I had zero experience. I knew the process was very, *very* tedious. *What about my employment half-life? Wouldn't I get bored and quit? Stop it! That's wrong thinking. I have to land an animation job first before I could even think of quitting. So, there're two far more critical questions. How do I become an animator? Where do I have to go?*

In 1978 only three places in America had animation studios operating on an industrial scale: Los Angeles, Orlando, and New York City. *Shit! I can't move my family to one of those cities without having a job. But who'd hire me without animation experience?* This looked like an impasse I'd have to consider later, so I'd move on to something else. *Okay, let's say I got hired. If so, what would I actually do as an animator?*

With no experience, I'd start at the bottom as an in-betweener. I knew lead animators created the primary action keyframes, which may happen every few seconds or so. Then the assistant animator draws a few intermediate frames. Finally, it's the in-betweener's job to draw all the remaining frames between each keyframe. This is a purely mechanical process. It requires interpreting ever-so-slight changes between keyframe positions and accurately drawing each in-between frame with a pencil. I sighed. *That sounds terribly boring.* I moved on. *What about an inker?* That meant carefully tracing each frame's pencil drawing with ink onto a transparent cell. *That seems even more mindless. What if I was a painter?* Then I'd have to fill in each cell with a paintbrush, following a specific color-by-number scheme. *I couldn't imagine painting forty hours a week, as if it was a coloring book.* I felt discouraged.

There was another serious problem. *I'm a creative guy.* None of those positions required much creativity. I'd be a technical artist executing someone else's creative instructions. In an animation studio, few people actually get to be genuinely creative. Experienced people would kill for those jobs. *To get to the next level, I'd have to work for years in a studio. How could I possibly convince my family to move someplace where I'd likely get bored to tears and quit?* This was an incredibly depressing realization.

It was clear, animating to music—or any animation—at a studio was ruled out. After all, how much of that work was there for someone of my limited qualifications? Depressed but undaunted, I returned to the well of crazy ideas and pulled out the next one.

Why not do it on my own? That was a natural question since I'd been a self-motivated freelance artist. As I considered producing cartoons on my own, immediately, the scope of the process stopped me. *Sure, I could animate, draw, and paint all my own cells. But how long would it take?* That wouldn't be economical. Besides, I was broke. That option was beyond laughable. Now I was even more depressed, having exhausted the possible lines of reasoning to achieve my dream career. It would remain just that—a dream. *No!* I refused. *There's got to be something.*

The holed muffler blatted loudly and painfully in my ears. My mind, immersed in the white noise, lay open, waiting for inspiration. The crucible effects had heated the metal of my mind to white-hot, which set upon God's anvil. The hammer dropped, striking the metal. Instantly, an image materialized in my brain.

It looked like a box … a three-dimensional object … a line drawing … rotating. *What is it?* I reached deeper into my mind to focus and identify the source of that image. *Yes!*

In high school, I had the opportunity to watch the movie *2001: A Space Odyssey* every Saturday night for twelve weeks straight. I'd been totally stunned and consumed by the movie's visual production value, enthralled by the futuristic technology, especially the visual screens, displaying dynamic, colored graphical information. But my eureka moment had burst forth from that single three-dimensional display on the HAL 9000—the spaceship's onboard computer. HAL showed a communication device as an animated blueprint, a 3D object rotating in space. I immediately recognized the possibilities. I'd used blueprints to create colored, perspective architectural renderings of proposed buildings.

Suddenly, the hammer struck again. I had a quantum leap of

consciousness. *If a computer can create a 3D line drawing of an object and rotate it in space, what if the computer could apply a colored surface over the drawing? A computer could produce animated 3D-cartoons!* Robert was right. God spoke to me at that moment through HAL's display screen. I had *The* Plan. *I'll make cartoons with computers!*

Creative possibilities and fantastic animated images flooded my mind, but this revelation posed new questions. *What will I produce? Who will buy it?* Another brain flash! Cable TV, an emerging new medium. *If I can create short animations synchronized to music, I could sell them as fillers between cable TV programming.* I believed this was a viable market and answered the question of who will buy my animations.

Armed with an answer for Kate, calm settled sublimely over me. Knowing The Plan was finally in hand, and that I'd figured out what to do and who'd buy it—

The calm abruptly disappeared in ripples of doubt, as if someone suddenly threw a boulder into a tranquil pond.

Sure, I had a great idea—but so is antigravity. Reality check. The critical question faced me. *What do I know about computers?* All I knew was from watching *2001: A Space Odyssey* and *Star Trek.* My only direct experience using this technology was a pocket calculator. To make The Plan work, I'd have to figure out technical and mathematical complexities, not to mention getting my hands on a computer.

Concerned? Yes. Discouraged? No. This was my dream. It was worth figuring out. My commercial art career began under similar circumstances. After I dropped out of college, I heard you could make a good living producing architectural renderings. It sounded like a good idea. I knew how to read blueprints, understood perspective, and the hand skills to pull it off. Then, as now, reality slammed home. I'd never actually created a rendering and had no clue how to do it. However, persistence is a powerful force. I figured it out and launched myself into the unpredictable world of commercial art.

I did it before, and I'll do it again. I taught myself illustration, rendering, and graphic arts. Yet doubt niggled in my mind. *I never got higher than a D in math.* It was hardly the skillset to embark on a new career in making cartoons with computers. *No, damn it!* I believed God revealed The Plan for a reason. I was confident I could acquire the knowledge and technical resources.

"I've got it!" I shouted.

"Got what?" Barney asked.

"The Plan!"

"What is it?"

"I'll tell you later when we don't have to shout." Secure knowing I'd avoid murder when I eventually reached home, I relaxed for the remainder of my drive with Barney.

◈

From today's perspective, it's easy to say what's the big deal. Today, computer graphics animation and special effects are ubiquitous, but that was April 1978. Back then, flight simulators and computer-aided design—neither of which I'd ever heard of—were the primary uses of computer graphics visualization. The first *Star Wars* movie hit the screens in 1977. Except for the Death Star's technical readout, there were no computer graphics used in that production. In those days, special effects used miniatures and optical film compositing—a non-digital, analog process, and animation was still hand-drawn. In fact, the 3D object from *2001* was animated by hand. They used no computer graphics. There I was, living in Marlow, New Hampshire, with the Internet still two decades away, and utterly unaware of any existing computer graphics technology. Despite my lack of knowledge, connections, or opportunities, somehow, I now had The Plan; I'd pulled it out of nothing. You can call it whatever you wish—I call it Divine Inspiration.

Chapter 15

Explanation

WE REACHED YOUNGSTOWN IN THE AFTERNOON. Barney said, "We better drive to Sue's place before we drop off the car." *Sue? I hope this won't be like his appearance in Brownsville.* To my relief, when we arrived, Sue greeted Barney with open arms. She looked about thirty with medium length dark hair and large expressive eyes. He asked her, "Can I get you to follow us when we drop off the Fiat so you can bring us back here?"

"Anything for you, Barney." She grinned.

When we reached the Fiat's final destination, Barney handed the keys to the owner. "I guess you heard how loud the car is. I'm sorry, but the muffler gave out in Huston."

"And you drove all that far like that?" Her face looked sad. "Well, don't worry. I'm just happy to have my car back."

Driving back to Sue's place, she suggested, "It's kind of late. Why doesn't Randy come back with us so he can get some sleep? That way, you can drop him off in the morning, and he can get a fresh start."

"Your call," Barney said, looking at me in the back seat.

Despite being anxious to get home, the thought of sleeping horizontally on a motionless couch in her quiet apartment overrode my anxiety. Besides, it would be dark soon, and I couldn't face waiting for rides that night. "I think that's a great idea."

When we reached Sue's apartment, I called Kate. "I'm in

Youngstown—"

"Have you figured out a plan?" Her voice was terse. She didn't even give me a chance to ask how she and the kids were doing.

At least I was prepared and answered confidently, "Yes!"

That stopped her for a moment. "Really?"

"Yes."

"What is it?" Her voice sounded excited for the first time since I left.

"Listen, I'm exhausted, and it's too complicated to tell you now." I wanted the pleasure of personally seeing her reaction when I told her The Plan. "Also, the guy I drove with offered me a place to sleep tonight since it's getting late." I thought it was better to tell her it was Barney's suggestion. "Barney will drop me off at the highway first thing in the morning."

"When will you be home?"

"It's about 600 miles. If I was driving, about ten hours, but I can't count on that. Late tomorrow night if I'm lucky—"

"You better try."

I didn't know how to answer without an argument. "I'll certainly do the best I can because I don't want to spend another night on the road." Before she could respond, I asked, "How are you doing? How are the kids?"

"It's complicated. I don't want to talk about it over the phone."

I see. Tit-for-tat. "Okay. I love you. See you soon."

Under the circumstances, I couldn't expect a civil conversation with Kate. Now that I'd figured out The Plan, I'd had more cycles to think about her and the family and how hard it must have been during my absence. *Soon it'll be over, and I'll be there to help out.*

"Pizza's here," Sue called out from the kitchen.

Mmmm, pizza! Then I remembered pizza with Eddie and the strange triangle in Phoenix, which seemed so very long ago, and I couldn't help wonder how that played out. I thanked God I'd eat this pizza under far better circumstances.

As we ate, drank beer, and sampled more of Barney's Tai stick, he filled Sue in on the highlights of his past five years. When he finished describing the drive from Tucson, he looked at me and asked, "Hey, didn't you say you figured out your plan?"

"What plan?" Sue asked.

Before I could answer, Barney jumped in. "You see this guy?" Barney grabbed and shook my shoulder. "He's much crazier than he looks. You know why he's here?"

"How could I possibly know?" Sue replied and took another drink from her beer.

"This crazy idiot," Barney pointed at me, "convinced his pregnant wife to let him hitchhike from New Hampshire to Tucson and leave her alone for a month with three kids and a one-year-old baby—"

"No way!" Sue slammed her beer on the table and looked at me like I was from Mars. "I'd have killed you," she said. "You're terrible!"

I smiled. Despite being too full, too high, and too relaxed, I had to push back. "If you must know, here's the story." During the next beer and a few more slices of pizza, I told Sue about my reasons for leaving and related the high points of my journey.

"You're some kind of nut," Sue said with a horrified look. "If you don't have a damn good plan, she's gonna kill you." It was the standard prediction.

"Why does everyone need to tell me that?" I complained.

"Enough!" Barney cried out. "So, give. What's this grand plan you cooked up last night?" Barney rocked back in his chair and drank from his beer bottle.

I grinned like the Cheshire Cat. "I'm going to make cartoons with computers and sell them to cable TV." I looked back and forth between them, unnerved by their seeming lack of reaction. I could cut the silence with a knife. They looked like waxworks characters with permanent glassy-eyed stares.

Barney spoke first. “That’s your plan?”

“That’s what you’re gonna tell your wife?” Sue exclaimed.

Barney came forward in his chair. “What the hell are you talking about? My Tai stick’s good shit, but it ain’t LSD, ‘cause you sound like you’re hallucinating.” He waved his hands dismissively. “Cartoons! Computers! You *are* nuts.”

“I don’t know if you should let this guy loose on the street,” Sue cautioned with a straight face. “He’s out of his mind.”

As I experienced their reaction to The Plan, I quickly realized God was good to me, providing the opportunity to test my idea first. I was sure Kate would have a similar reaction, so I definitely needed some practice. I took a long pull on my beer, gently set the bottle down, clasped my hands, and rested on my elbows. “Between the blown muffler and your Tai stick, creating an altered state …” I explained my thought process and the concept. Sue and Barney were willing and interested soundingboards and asked many questions.

“If you don’t know anything about computers,” Sue asked, “how on earth will you figure it out?”

“I’ll have to find people who do and learn all that I can from them.”

“Where?” Barney asked.

“There’s a college in Keene. I’ll go to the computer department and find someone.”

“What are you going to do about money?” Sue queried.

That one stopped me. I took another sip. “I’ll start a business and find investors.” That sounded plausible to me.

“What do you know about business?” Sue pressed.

“I suppose about as much as I know about computers—”

“Man, you’re fucked!” Barney said and then laughed at me.

“I’ll learn.”

“How?” Sue asked.

“I’ll find books and read about it. I’m sure I can do it.”

“Oh, brother,” she said. “You may as well tell your wife you’re gonna fly to the moon and open a cheese factory. You know you’re a dead man. Divorced at a minimum.”

“Yeah,” Barney added. “Your plan’s as holey as Swiss cheese.”

“You better have some better answers before you get home,” Sue warned.

“I suppose you’re right. I’ll sleep on it and give it some thought tomorrow.”

It was a pleasure to be sleeping on a couch and away from the horrible exhaust noise that assaulted me from Texas to Ohio. My ears no longer rang continuously, and I listened to the din of late-night traffic in the city beyond the window. Excitement trumped exhaustion, knowing I’d likely be home within twenty-four hours. Unable to sleep, the pattern on the ceiling from the streetlight below drew my attention. For the first time in a long while, I didn’t feel scared. The worry of returning home empty-handed was behind me. I’d survived the dangerous trip to the goldfields but, there was no gold in my pockets—I think I had eight bucks. I hadn’t struck it rich, at least not an immediate reward, but I’d found paydirt where I could stake my claim for a brighter future.

I thought it interesting that Barney and Sue didn’t mention anything about abandoning my family or that I was selfish and self-centered. Crazy, yes. But It was clear to them my quest was motivated by love and responsibility. After I explained The Plan, Sue had asked, “Why did you have to travel 6,500 miles to get away from a noisy household, only to figure out the solution in a deafening car?” It was a fair question and made me think of Dorothy in the *Wizard of Oz*. She had the power to return home at any moment, but instead, she endured her dangerous quest to appreciate better what she had before she left.

Like Dorothy, I felt there was no place like home, but that hadn’t been the question. It wasn’t that I needed to get away to appreciate what I had. I needed to get away from my life constraints at home and think clearly to make a better home for my family. Perhaps The Plan was there all the time, and I just didn't see it. But I think I needed the crucible's intense heat to reduce the ore of my thoughts and release pure gold. I required the exhaustion of the journey and the relentless sound of the Fiat to bring my mind to the point, whereas Robert said, "To listen more carefully." Maybe I hadn't found my guardian spirit, as Judd suggested. However, I did affirm my belief that God was, in fact, looking out for me.

My eyes closed, and sleep crept up on me. *I'm almost home*. Then I cringed at the idea of spending another moment hitchhiking. I tried to say *It's just one more day*, but I feared the road, the last barrier to my homecoming. I fell asleep with unsettling thoughts. However, I'd made my bed. It was my choice to make the journey, and I had no right to complain. I was outright scared at having to stand on the highway again, even for a day.

Chapter 16

Encounter

THE NEXT MORNING BARNEY AND I DROVE TO THE ENTRANCE RAMP FOR I-80 EAST, aiming me toward New York City. I sat in the car, reluctant to get back on the road with my little sign. Barney handed me a lit joint. "Maybe this will help."

When we finished, I said, "Thanks for the ride that got me this far. Despite the muffler, I had a great time with you."

"Me too. It's not often I meet someone as nutty as me who isn't a total flake." He grinned. "Best of luck. Stay safe, and I hope your wife buys your bullshit." He laughed as I got out of the car, set my pack on the ground, and then reached in and shook his hand goodbye. I watched him drive away, then turn toward the entrance ramp.

Low clouds, the color of slate, felt oppressive, bearing down with the weight of water, promising to unload on me at any time. I hoped to get a ride before the rain and beyond the New York metropolitan area before dark. After my Memphis experience, I didn't want to be stuck at night in New York City, trying to make my way through. It was about four-hundred miles to New York, and even with a continuous ride, it would take over six hours. I hoped with a little luck; maybe I'd get a ride from someone heading to Boston.

For the first time in weeks, I stood alone at a typical entrance ramp, holding my cardboard sign with bold letters: NH. Even if people thought it was New Haven, Connecticut, that would be an excellent destination.

Within half an hour, the first sprinkles spattered my face, then drizzle, and finally, a steady light rain. It was a bad start. Hitchhiking was awful enough, but being wet made it far worse. People were reluctant to invite a wet stranger into their vehicle. I walked to the top of the ramp to reach the highway. A steady stream of traffic passed. The shooshing of wet tires on the pavement sounded like the surf rolling in and out of the beach. I waited more than an hour for my first ride, which took me less than twenty-five miles. That's how the day went—long wait times for short rides. As I headed east, the storm followed, so the cold rain was nonstop. My hat was soaked. Rivulets streamed down my trenchcoat, dripping off the hem like rain from an awning. I was miserable. It took nearly eight hours to reach the New Jersey border as the day came to a close, and the wet night descended quickly. It was still over eighty miles to get past New York City.

The first decent ride took me about fifty miles. It was 10:30 p.m. when the driver dropped me off at Parsippany, New Jersey, within thirty miles of New York. The rain was relentless, coming in great sheets of droplets, glittering in the streetlights, spattering the ground, looking like some huge bubbling pan.

I was tired of waiting on the highway and wanted a hot drink. Just off the exit ramp, I saw a restaurant and reached into my pocket and pulled out my money. Three singles, a five-dollar bill, and some loose change filled my wet hand. I started walking and decided to get something to eat.

As I approached the eatery, a large red neon sign announced DINER. A car door popped open, and a young guy about my age emerged from the passenger side of a silver Firebird. He stepped into the light that streamed from the diner's large windows facing the wet parking lot and asked, "Hey man, you need a ride?" He was about my height, but a slighter frame, his short hair was red, and a stringy mustache barely covered his upper lip.

"Where are you going?" I asked as the rain fell harder.

The guy regarded me with cold blue eyes. "Where are *you* goin'?" He wore a green army jacket, ratty jeans and held a cigarette between two nicotine-stained fingers.

"I'm headed for New Hampshire."

"Where's that?"

"North," was the extent of my geography lesson. "I'd be really happy just to get the other side of New York."

"We can do that," he said, smiling and beckoning me to the car.

"That'd be great." I was excited about being offered a ride beyond the city.

The guy opened the door and pulled the seat forward. "Get in the back. I'll put your pack in the front between the driver and me."

I ducked down to climb in the back when, much to my surprise, I saw two girls sitting there. When I hesitated, the pair scooted to either side, giggling as they patted the seat between them. "Don't be shy," said the blonde behind the driver.

I squeezed myself in. My long legs pulled up nearly to my chest. The inside of the car smelled like cigarettes, cheap perfume, and body odor. I smiled at the blonde with short hair, maybe twenty, skinny, and overly made up. She wore a faded denim jacket and jeans. Her mouth rhythmically clicked as she smiled and chewed a wad of gum. On the other side was a girl who looked about the same age with long dark hair, dark eyes, and a round face. Her mouth worked mercilessly on a piece of gum, and she tried to smile at me. Thick blue eye shadow covered her lids over green eyes. She was heftier, and her skintight jeans clung to her legs, giving them the effect of being poured into the denim. "Hi, ladies," I said. They replied with girlish giggles.

The guy who invited me shoved back the seat, firmly pinning me in place, locked between the two girls. My pack was against my knees, and I felt extremely uncomfortable. The guy put his elbow on the back of his seat, turned around, and grinned at me. The driver also turned to look back at me from a stubbly face with deep-set brown eyes. His hair was stringy brown, and it brushed his shoulders. He dressed like the other guy but looked noticeably larger than his friend. They just stared for what seemed like a long uncomfortable time. The girls giggled again and broke the heavy silence.

"Where're you goin'?" asked the driver.

"Connecticut." I figured I'd keep it simple. "Your friend told me you were going that way."

"Okay." The grin vanished. "You got any money for gas?"

RED ALERT! My stomach knotted as I looked at the passenger, who still grinned. It was very creepy. For the first time during the entire journey, I was seriously scared. It wasn't like crossing the Mississippi when I feared unintentionally getting brushed from the bridge by a great impersonal truck. *What the hell have I done?* I worried. Like some kind of stupid moron, I'd allowed myself to get locked in the back seat, wedged behind my pack. There was no escape from the car unless they allowed me to leave. Something in their tone of voice, their eyes, and the crooked grin on the passenger's face told me I was in the company of people best to avoid. Eddie Long may have been on a parole violation, but he didn't scare me. *I wish he were here right now.*

My hesitation prompted the passenger to ask me again more aggressively, "I'm sure you've got some gas money for us. Don't you?" All the grins and smiles faded.

It was my turn to smile, hoping to convince them I wasn't scared. I took the prudent course of action. "I'm about tapped out, but here," I pulled the crumpled five from my pocket. "Other than some change, it's all I have." I held out the bill, and the driver snatched it out of my hand. "Since you guys are taking me to the other side of New York, I think it's fair." The two guys laughed as the driver backed out of the parking lot and drove to the gas pump, where he jumped out.

"Since you're helping us, man, you deserve a reward," said the passenger.

"The ride's reward enough." I forced another smile.

"Nope, you deserve somethin' real nice." He grinned and said, "Go on, girls, show 'im what I mean."

The girls had stopped giggling when the guys asked for money. I looked at the blonde, wondering what he was talking about. The next moment her arm roughly circled my neck, pulled me close, and mashed her mouth against mine. I felt her tongue knocking at my lips. I was stunned, but before I could recover, the other girl said, "My turn." She pushed the blonde away and spun me around, applying a similar kiss.

I could see the passenger leering at me from the corner of my eye. Then he said, "Hey man, don't get too carried away with the ladies. Just 'cause they're bein' nice, don't you go takin' advantage of our girlfriends."

Take advantage? They were assaulting me while the psycho moron watched. I feared any moment he'd pull out a knife or a gun. I gently pushed the girl away and tried to remain calm, hoping none of them saw me trembling. I smiled again, looked at each girl, and said, "Thank you, ladies." Then I smiled at the passenger, doing my best to show my appreciation while hiding my terror.

The girls sat back, giggling as the driver returned to the car. Looking back at me, he asked, "What's so fuckin' funny."

"The girls were just thanking our guest for the gas money," his friend chuckled.

With squealing tires, we pulled away from the gas station and onto the highway. "*Pain will come back to you*," suddenly refrained in my head. It was dreadfully silent in the car. No radio. No conversation. Just the sound of the driver manually shifting through the gears of his muscle car, the wipers, and the hiss of tires on the wet road. I tried to see where we were going from my limited view through the windshield. It was a relief when I saw a sign proclaim: I-80 New York. My relief evaporated when the driver veered to the right, driving under the sign for I-280 south to Newark. *Newark? What the fuck is going on?* "Shouldn't we be on I-80?"

I asked as neutrally as possible.

"We're takin' a shortcut," the driver laughed and glared at me in the rearview mirror.

I felt sick. I feared it might be a shortcut to a bad end. We cruised down I-280 through the dark rainy night. I was completely disoriented and had no idea where I was. For a while, it was rural, dark trees lining the highway, but things became more built up and eventually looked quite urban.

It was nearly midnight as I watched them turn onto the Garden State Parkway heading south toward Union. *Some shortcut. They're taking me in the opposite direction.* I forced myself to remain calm despite a sickening fear of where the ride might end. The passenger looked around and seemed disappointed that I appeared so calm. I smiled, trying to look as if I was enjoying myself. *You stupid fuckin' moron. Stop the car and let me out*, I thought behind my false grin. He turned to the driver and said, "Looks like he's havin' too good a time. We should prob'ly let him out." I was ecstatic at those words.

The car suddenly pulled over to the shoulder. The passenger jumped out, tossed my pack on the pavement, and pulled the seat forward. I needed no encouragement and quickly scrambled out without saying goodbye to either of the ladies. I stood on the shoulder, my knees shaking. As the passenger got back in the car, they all laughed and sped away on the rain-soaked highway.

I felt marvelous after escaping the psycho mobile, though my whole body shook violently. I was so relieved that I hadn't noticed my surroundings or that it was still raining. All I cared about was that I was out of that car and unhurt. Then it struck me. Where I stood, the Parkway was below grade. I was in a concrete trench surrounded by walls twenty feet tall, with no exit in sight. The bozos had dropped me off at a terrible spot. I had no clue where I was. Making things that much more miserable, the rain fell harder. Since I didn't know where I was, all I could do was backtrack to the I-80 interchange.

To head back north, I had to cross the empty highway and start walking. A few vehicles passed but didn't stop. I walked over a mile before a delivery truck picked me up and drove me about twenty-five miles, and dropped me off along the rural stretch of the highway. I didn't know how far back it was to I-80, so I continued to walk in the rain.

At 3:00 a.m., the highway was empty, and no cars had passed by during the previous hour. The initial euphoria of escaping the psycho mobile had long since worn off. I was wet, tired, and depressed. I couldn't keep, "*Pain will come back to you*," out of my head, and God seemed to ignore all my requests. I feared being stuck on the spot until after dawn when traffic would pick up. I sat on my backpack. I needed sleep, but that was impossible.

After a while, through the sound of the rain, I heard an approaching vehicle some distance away. I stood up, hoping whoever was driving at this hour would pity me. "Please stop, please stop," I repeated over and over after the headlights appeared. My heart leaped when the car slowed and pulled onto the shoulder. I was exuberant that someone finally stopped—

Suddenly, red gumballs flashed and strobed. Shafts of light from the headlights, filled with sparkling rain, illuminated my wet and pathetic figure. I didn't care that it was the cops. In fact, I welcomed the officers questioning me while sitting in the back of the cruiser and subsequently to be taken to a warm, dry police station.

Both doors opened, and two officers slowly walked up to me. Standing in the headlights on either side, I saw they were New Jersey State Police officers. However, unlike the starched uniformed Tennessee trooper, these two looked like rent-a-cops. Barney Fife from *Andy of Mayberry* came to mind. They were both skinny, gawky, and their uniforms looked like they didn't fit. Their peaked hats with black leather visors were tilted way back and cocked to one side of their heads. Their appearance looked slaphappy and comical. However, their attitude was far from it. One of them immediately began to frisk me while the other cop started to rummage in my backpack.

"You got any drugs?" asked the cop as he frisked me. But his attitude made me think they wanted to score rather than to bust me. When he finished patting me down, he asked, "Where are you going?"

"New Hampshire."

The other cop pulled from my bag a six-inch metal hoop, and suspiciously asked, "What's this?"

"My embroidery hoop."

That stunned them both into a silent stupor. The cop held it, turning it in the light, trying to fathom if it was some sort of martial arts weapon.

"Let's see some ID," the other cop demanded, thrusting out his wet hand. I handed it to him. He didn't even look at it as they returned to the cruiser, leaving me out in the rain.

You bastards! Why don't you invite me into the dry warmth of your squad car?

They ran my license as I stood in the rain. After about ten minutes, the cop on the passenger side rolled down his window and motioned to me. "Get over here."

I approached and bent over. "Yes?"

He shoved my license at me. "You need to get off the highway."

I looked around as I was between exits and had no place to go. "Where?" I hoped they might offer me a ride to the next exit.

"You figure it out." He rolled up the window, and they sped off into the rainy night.

"Thanks for the help!" I shouted as I hoisted my backpack and started walking, hoping to reach an exit soon. I didn't want to be there when they returned. After walking for about twenty minutes, I heard a vehicle coming from behind. I was too tired to look back and hold up my sign. Suddenly a horn honked. I turned and saw a truck sitting there, the windshield wipers sweeping back and forth, so I walked to his door.

"Want a ride?" the driver asked.

Silently, I went to the other side and climbed inside. "Thanks," was all I could manage.

"You're soaked. What are you doing out here?"

I explained the events since the psycho mobile picked me up. My story gave him a great laugh. "It's out of my way, but after that, I'll take you back to I-80".

Chapter 17

Return

I WAS BACK ON COURSE. The sky off to the east grew light, and the rain had mostly tapered off. I looked at the entrance ramp and highway ahead of me. Then I looked at the gas station and diner across the street. At that moment, my strength gave out. It was four days and four nights since I left Tucson. Despite the drive-away car and the previous night in Youngstown, the extra distance and the blown muffler took a lot out of me. Terror in the Firebird and the subsequent aftermath had drained me completely. Somehow, I couldn't face trying to hitchhike through New York City. I had three dollars and some loose change. I crossed the street to get a hot drink.

My hands clasped the mug as I sipped hot tea. I tried to figure out what to do next as the world grew lighter and the morning progressed. Commuter traffic streamed east to New York, but I couldn't move and do what was required to beg for a ride. At that moment, I wished I were farther north on I-84 in a more rural location. Hitching into the city was more than I could handle. At 9:00, I called Kate.

"Where are you?"

"New Jersey, just west of New York."

"I was worried about you." That was the first sign of concern I'd heard from her since I left.

I gave her the gist of my journey from Youngstown with no details and explained how exhausted I was. "I'm not sure how I'm going to get home at this point."

She thought for a moment. "What's the number of the phone booth? I'm going to make a call. I'll get back to you soon."

I hung up the phone and waited. Five minutes later, Kate rang back. "I called some old family friends of my parents in Demarest—Betty, and John. I talked with Betty. She said if you can get to their house, she'll feed you and give you money for a bus ticket back to Keene." Kate gave me their address and directions.

It took a moment for the news to sink in. Then a wave of relief swept over me. "That's great news. Thanks, dear. I'll call you when I get there."

After I hung up, I couldn't imagine how I'd make it to Demarest. I saw a VW Bug drive up to the gas pumps and suddenly remembered Judd from Englewood, who'd asked me to call on the way back. I searched for his number in my wallet and dumped some change into the phone. *I hope the hell you're home.*

Three rings and he picked up. He sounded sleepy. "Hello?"

"Judd?" I tried not to sound too anxious. "This is Randy."

"Hey! Good to hear from you. Where are you?"

I explained my situation.

He was very cheerful. "Tell me what exit you're at. I'll come get you and take you to Demarest."

I hung up the phone, stepped out of the booth, stood outside a moment, and broke down and cried with relief. I was glad I released it before Judd arrived. If not, I would have lost it for sure when he picked me up.

It took him about a half-hour to get there. When he saw me, Judd said, "You look like shit." That confirmed just how I felt. I climbed in and handed him the address. He knew the area where Betty and John lived. As we headed for Demarest, which was just north of Englewood, I could barely stay awake. Another half-hour later, we pulled into Betty's driveway. I got out and knocked on their door while Judd waited in the VW.

Betty greeted me at the door. She was stunned. Kate hadn't prepared her for how out of it I was. "Come in. Please come in." The woman was in her late sixties, and as she warmly welcomed me into her home, she waved Judd to come in.

"I bet you'd like to get out of those wet clothes and take a shower," she offered. "I'll run your clothes through the dryer. You can wear the robe hanging on the door."

"That'd be wonderful."

"While you're showering, I'll fix you some breakfast."

Judd followed me to the bathroom, where I handed him my clothes. As I showered, I could barely stay on my feet under the hot water, but the feeling was glorious. The water streamed over my long hair, and I thought about the psychos in the Firebird. "Thank you, God," I said, feeling grateful for making it out alive.

A short while later, I entered the kitchen, where Betty and Judd sat at the table drinking coffee. The smell of bacon mixed with coffee greeted me, along with Betty asking, "Feel better?"

Wrapped in a plush navy bathrobe, I sat down. "I'm wonderful, thanks to you." As I ate bacon and fried eggs with toast, I talked about my journey. Her face revealed a range of emotions as she and Judd asked me different questions. Much to my relief, neither of them asked me if I'd come up with a plan, and no one suggested that Kate would kill me. When I finished, Betty said, "You poor dear. Thank God you're safe. I don't know how you did it." She looked sad but then smiled. She stood up. "Let me see if your clothes are dry."

Judd stared at me over the rim of his coffee cup, then set it down. "You're a very lucky son-of-a-bitch."

"Lucky that you picked me up in Greenfield," I replied.

"When you're ready, I'll run you down to Port Authority," Judd offered as Betty returned with my clothes.

She handed them to me and said, "There's a bus leaving from Port

Authority for Keene in a couple of hours. It should get you there around 6:00 p.m."

I got dressed and then called Kate to tell her my schedule and when to pick me up. We didn't talk much, knowing I'd be home that evening. As I arranged my pack and got ready to leave, Betty handed me some money. "This will cover the bus ticket and get a bite to eat before you leave."

I took the bills and squeezed her hand warmly, feeling overcome, and nearly burst out crying. "You're too kind. I don't know how I can ever thank you. I'll send you some money—"

She pushed my hand away. "Don't you dare even think about it. I'm only too happy to help you. Just tell Kate I love her."

Judd and I got in the VW as Betty waved goodbye from her front door. A few minutes later, we headed for the George Washington Bridge. "Sounds like you had quite an adventure."

"I'm glad it's about over."

"So, tell me," he asked. "What's your plan?" As we crossed the GW bridge and drove down the West Side Highway, I explained what happened to me while driving through Columbus. He listened to me tell him what I planned to do and finally said, "Looks like you had a successful vision quest."

"I don't think I found my spirit guide."

"You don't say." He chuckled. "Well, I don't know anything about technology or computers, but it sounds like a fascinating idea."

"Do you think my wife will find it believable?"

He laughed and shook his head. "No."

Judd let me out at the 42nd Street entrance to the Port Authority bus terminal. "Thanks again for your help on both ends of my trip. I don't know what I'd have done without you today."

He shook my hand and smiled. "Glad I could help. Besides, I needed to hear about your vision quest."

I waved as he drove away, blending into the dense Manhattan traffic. I went inside, got my ticket, and waited at the gate until they called people to board the bus. When I finally got on and sat down, knowing it was the final leg of my trip, I was never so happy at the idea of getting back to my overcrowded house in Marlow, surrounded by all the commotion and noise of my family.

As the bus pulled out of Port Authority, I sat next to the window, lazily watching the city slide past as we made our way to I-95 north toward New Haven, Connecticut. I didn't see much of the trip after we left Manhattan until I woke up just north of Springfield, Massachusetts. I was about an hour from Keene and the end of my journey. With such a short distance to go, it felt like nothing compared to the miles and miles of Texas I'd driven through. In the late afternoon sun, I saw that spring had arrived. The grass was lush, and new leaves with their subtly varied shades of green covered the trees. I knew it would be colder in Marlow, but I didn't care. I looked forward to bringing in some wood and stoking the stove.

I reflected on 6.500 miles traveled between one corner of the country to another. Walking across the Mississippi seemed so long ago. As I wondered what happened with Eddie Long, and Julie-Sue, I grinned and shook my head. I thought about Sundance and his rage, wondering if he pounded Richard and brought Sunflower and Venus back to Albany. I almost laughed out loud When I recalled Barney's greeting in Brownsville. I shuddered, thinking about how lucky I was to have survived the previous night with those sickos in the psycho mobile. I knew I'd never hitchhike again. But my ride with Robert was fresh in my mind as I counted my blessings. I realized, despite the problems, discomfort, and abject terror, God, had looked out for me. I was returning safely to my family, and God had indeed helped me with The Plan. I thought about my idea, and the excitement energized me. I only hoped Kate would be satisfied with The Plan.

◈

The bus pulled into Keene right on time, and when I stepped off, I saw Kate waiting in the Dodge. I went to the van and threw my pack in the back. It was a well-practiced move. I climbed into the passenger seat, as I had so many times before, and still felt like a hitchhiker. I shut the door, smiled at Kate, leaned over, and we embraced and kissed. Then she gently pushed me away and asked, "What's your plan?"

I sat back, a broad smile covering my face as I regarded her with confidence. I proclaimed, "I'm going to make cartoons with computers and sell them to cable TV." I waited for her response.

Kate stared blankly. She didn't say a word, then furrowed her brow, tried to say something, but stopped. She turned away from me, and as we drove out of the parking lot, she asked, "So how was your trip?"

I knew I'd have to wait until morning to explain The Plan, but I recounted my adventure as we headed back up Rt. 10 towards home. I got a mixed reaction from her. She laughed at Sundance and Eddie, showed concern about the Mississippi, and was genuinely upset about the psycho mobile.

It was about 7:00 when we pulled into our driveway in the middle of Marlow. At that moment, I felt like Dorothy because there was no place like home. When I got out of the van, I saw David and Mike wrestling in the living room through the lighted windows. Before I opened the door, I paused to listen to the commotion and was very happy. Happy to be alive and home with the family that I'd missed. No, I hadn't dwelled on them as much as one might think. I had other things on my mind. Things I'd hoped would improve our lot in life. As I stepped into the warmth of the house, almost automatically, I looked down at the boy's feet and saw their shoes. I regarded them with ambivalence, no longer terrified by them, as I'd survived worse terrors and would soon embark on the next phase of my quest to support my wife and kids.

Epilogue

I REMEMBER WHEN CAMPING WITH MY PARENTS AS A KID IN THE 1960S, how my Dad and I would sit up alone by the fire, watching it burn away to shimmering coals under the brilliant stars. He'd do most of the talking, which usually turned into reminiscing about his past during the Second World War, as a celestial navigator for Air Transport Command. When he spoke about those days, some twenty years earlier, he often commented, "It seems like it happened to a different person."

As I grew older, I better understood what he meant. My adventure was over forty years ago. Yes, I feel like it happened to a different person because four decades will change anybody. Yet, I still feel much the same. My dedication and sense of responsibility toward my family have not diminished. The impulse that sent me on that quest is very much alive within me. However, I believe I'm much wiser and certainly more experienced. When asked if I'd do it again under the same circumstances, make that journey, knowing what I know now, the answer is always yes.

Of course, there's the obvious question. How did the Plan work out? Well … convoluted and unexpected. The quest was a pivotal event in my life, with far-reaching consequences. The telling of that saga and other wacky adventures will be the subject of future memoirs. However, I suppose it's not fair, leaving you to wonder what happened.

It turned out that my eureka moment about making cartoons with computers was a presage of an entirely new industry that has transformed entertainment, publishing, and communications. Somehow, I had tuned into something that was beyond my limited knowledge and experience at that time. So, how did that inspiration change my life?

I did create a new career and never went back to cutting cordwood, that is—for money. Of course, that was some years away from the time I returned with The Plan. In the meantime, we continued to struggle with money. I focused on my illustration and generated enough freelance work to improve our situation slightly.

During that summer, Jack came east to visit his family in New York. He swung by Marlow to see me in my natural habitat. It was a pleasant August afternoon, and Jack and my family were swimming in a river. The sunlight filtered through the green rustling leaves, sparkling on the flowing water. Jack, Kate, and I sat on the bank, watching the older kids splashing in the river. Kate was approaching her eighth month of pregnancy and looked it. Jack was taking it all in, watching David chase Michael through the water. "I see it with my own eyes but find it hard to believe you have a wife and four kids with another one on the way." He turned toward me and asked, "So, how's the new career thing going?"

Kate looked away. "It's difficult learning about computers in such a rural place." My frustration showed. "I can't seem to find any information about computer graphics at the college in Keene or even over at the University of New Hampshire."

Jack said, "Why don't you guys move to Tucson?"

I stared blankly. The concept had never crossed my mind, but the suggestion instantly brought up multiple ideas. *The U of A is a big university, and there's a great science library. I found freelance work in Tucson before, so I'd have a better chance in a large city.*

Kate looked at me, knowing I was deep in thought. I don't know if she grasped Jack's suggestion, but she asked, "What are you thinking? Whatever it is, it looks dangerous." She knew me too well.

"He's thinking about Tucson." Jack grinned.

"Tucson?" Kate stared at me. "You can't be serious."

When Jack suggested moving, I knew that was the answer. There was no way I could make things happen in tiny Marlow in rural New Hampshire. I saw all the benefits of executing The Plan in Tucson, but I knew that wouldn't sell Kate on such a radical concept as packing up and moving the family 2,600 miles to Tucson. I needed something Kate could immediately understand as a compelling reason. Michael ran screaming past us with David in hot pursuit, arms flailing like a monster, shouting and yelling as he bolted past. *That's it!* I took Kate's hand, looked into her eyes, and said, "A small house in a warm climate is much easier to deal with five kids than another winter in Marlow."

It was the winning argument, and Kate was on board with moving to Tucson. I'll leave that story to another *A Wild Ride* memoir. It was in Tucson that I taught myself how to program computers, became a computer graphics animator. That evolved into special effects designer and animator making videos and TV commercials. My self-acquired knowledge and experience also fulfilled another dream I once had.

I always wanted to work at a think tank. Despite no college degree and poor math skills, I worked at IBM Computer Science Research for over six years. I also published papers on computer graphics, video production, simulation, and training, presenting papers in the U.S. and Europe.

None of that would have been possible without the desperate jump into the crucible that transformed my life. However, an axiom of life is that everything comes at a price. I wish I could say it was all positive, but The Plan also set in motion events that produced considerable pain, much like that annoying refrain. In any event, this has just been one adventure in a wild ride that's been my life.

◈

Author's note: When I wrote this memoir, I couldn't remember the name of the song or the group responsible for *Pain will come back to you*. I tried to find the name of the song by searching the Internet for the refrain lyrics. Nothing. I thought that was very odd. Then one day, when shopping at the grocery store, I heard that familiar refrain. I wrote down the opening lines of the song and went home to search for it. It turns out it was Steely Dan's 1977 *Peg*. I listened to it, and there was the oh so familiar refrain. When I looked at the lyrics, much to my surprise, I discovered the refrain was actually, *PEG will come back to you*, not Pain. From that day in the motor home, I'd always heard pain, not Peg, until the moment of discovery. I guess, after all, maybe it was some sort of private message.

About the Author

"I WAS BORN IN TEXAS," RANDY KOONS PROCLAIMED ON HIS FOURTH BIRTHDAY, "BUT MY MOTHER WASN'T THERE." When all the adults laughed, Randy became a storyteller that day. It began a wild ride that has lasted a lifetime.

No, Randy's not a famous storyteller. His wild, unusual, humorous, and sometimes painful life includes an assortment of jobs such as underground copper miner, working at IBM's Computer Science Research, lumberjack, driller, and blaster. Randy's an illustrator, writer, and computer animator who made TV commercials in Minneapolis and on Madison Avenue. He helped design digital content creation tools at IBM Research and a computer-based incident command simulator for the National Fire Academy. Randy never graduated from college, but he's published and presented peer-reviewed technical papers in the US and Europe and has published short stories. He's a self-employed writer and animator and has run a creative writer's group for the past seven years.

Randy married twice, raised six kids, and along the way, has lived at 29 addresses in nine states. He currently lives with his wife in New Hampshire in a house that demands challenging DIY projects.

Randy's life experiences make for good storytelling, which he's capturing in a memoir series titled *A Wild Ride*. The first release in his series is *The Plan that Changed Everything*, which recounts the long fortuitous 6,500-mile journey that set him on an unlikely life course.

You can follow Randy on his blog at *www.a-wild-ride.com*.

Made in the USA
Middletown, DE
19 April 2021